RICHARD WRIGHT

CRITICAL STUDIES ON BLACK
LIFE AND CULTURE
(VOL. 18)

GARLAND REFERENCE LIBRARY
OF THE HUMANITIES
(VOL. 892)

CRITICAL STUDIES ON BLACK LIFE AND CULTURE
Professor Henry-Louis Gates, Advisory Editor

RICHARD WRIGHT
Myths and Realities

edited by
C. James Trotman

GARLAND PUBLISHING, INC. • NEW YORK & LONDON
1988

Library of Congress Cataloging-in-Publication Data

Richard Wright : myths and realities / [edited by] C. James Trotman.
    p. cm. — (Critical studies on Black life and culture ; vol.
18)   (Garland reference library of the humanities ; vol. 892)
    Papers of the Richard Wright Literary Symposium, held in Oct. 1985
at West Chester University, and sponsored by the English Dept.
    Includes bibliographies and index.
    ISBN 0-8240-7839-X (alk. paper)
    1. Wright, Richard, 1908-1960—Criticism and interpretation—
Congresses.   2. Afro-Americans in literature—Congresses.
I. Trotman, C. James, 1943- . II. Richard Wright Literary
Symposium (1985 : West Chester University) III. West Chester
University of Pennsylvania. English Dept. IV. Series. V. Series:
Critical studies on Black life and culture ; v. 18.
PS3545.R815Z817   1988
813.52—dc19   88-26012
                                               CIP

The front cover design is taken from an illustration of a door from Senufo, Ivory Coast, Boundiali region, reproduced in the Philadelphia Art Museum's catalog, *African Sculpture*, written by Allen Wardwell. The large doors of the Senufo are used to show the wealth and prestige of the important members of the community.

Robert L. Douglas's article, "Religious Orthodoxy and Skepticism in Richard Wright's *Uncle Tom's Children* and *Native Son*," is reprinted from *The Griot* 6, No. 3 (Fall 1987), with permission.

Michael Atkinson's article, "Richard Wright's 'Big Boy Leaves Home' and a Tale from Ovid: A Metamorphosis Transformed," is reprinted from *Studies in Short Fiction* 21, No. 23 (Summer 1987), with permission.

Printed on acid-free, 250-year-life paper
Manufactured in the United States of America

MARY ENID WILLIAMS TROTMAN
and
MARGARET BURR WALKER
WITH LOVE

. . . for in every human Breast, God has implanted a Principle, which we call Love of Freedom; it is impatient of oppression and pants for Deliverance—and by the Leave of our modern Egyptians I will assert that the same principle lives in us.

Phillis Wheatley to Rev. Samson Occom
in letter dated Feb. 11, 1774

. . . But I declare that the atrocity is really to Heaven daring and infernal, that I must say that God has commenced a course of exposition among the Americans, and the glorious and heavenly work will continue to progress until they learn to do justice.

from David Walker's *Appeal*, 1829

We would not for one moment check the outgrowth of any benevolent concern for the future welfare of the colored race in America or elsewhere; but in the name of reason and religion, we earnestly plead for justice before all else. Benevolence with justice is harmonious and beautiful; but benevolence without justice is a mockery.

Frederick Douglass, 1862

Fate is ourselves awake and asleep,
Fighting in the sky or armies in the earth,
Speeches, treaties, elections, hopes of heaven,
Preparations for hell. Fate is the collection plate

Of our sins and our loves—variety of coins,
Stored away or stolen by those fakirs
Who blame the plus or minus of our condition
On God or Devil or the sound of the sea.

Owen Dodson, "Definition"

Contents

Contributors

Michael Atkinson is Associate Professor of English and Comparative Literature at the University of Cincinnati in Cincinnati, Ohio.

Joseph Bodziock is Lecturer in English at Augsburg College in Minneapolis, Minnesota.

Elizabeth Ciner is Assistant Professor of English at Carleton College in Northfield, Minnesota.

Robert L. Douglas is Assistant Professor of Art History and Pan African Studies at the University of Louisville in Louisville, Kentucky.

Thomas Larson is Instructor of Composition and Literature at the University of San Diego in San Diego, California.

Paul Newlin is Associate Professor of English at the State University of New York at Stony Brook on Long Island, New York.

Alison Rieke is Instructor in English and Comparative Literature at the University of Cincinnati in Cincinnati, Ohio.

Marjorie Smelstor is Dean of the College of Sciences and Humanities at Ball State University in Muncie, Indiana.

Stephen Soitos teaches writing and literature courses at the University of Massachusetts in Amherst, Massachusetts.

C. James Trotman is Associate Professor of English at West Chester University in West Chester, Pennsylvania.

Robbie Jean Walker is Assistant Professor of English at Auburn University in Montgomery, Alabama.

Nagueyalti Warren is Chairperson of the English Department at Fisk University in Nashville, Tennessee.

Our Myths and Wright's Realities

C. James Trotman

This volume represents contemporary and fresh responses to the works of Richard Wright (1908–1960). The essays were first presented to the Richard Wright Literary Symposium in October 1985 on the campus of West Chester University in Pennsylvania. The collection includes several discussions on *Native Son* (1940), Wright's best known novel, the short fiction, particularly the works from *Uncle Tom's Children* (1938), the nonfiction, and the journalistic writings.

The audience for these papers is not limited by the academic setting in which they were given, for that would be a misleading view of who might enjoy this book. In general, the ideal reader for Wright derives satisfaction from forming positive correlations of a most significant kind: those between individual experiences and social orders, realities perceived and circumstances contrived, eternal truths and existential encounters, and of course literature and history, which is the correlation closest to Wright's work. Whatever its source, the correlation permits a range of responses from that of the informed scholar, the general reader, to the classroom teacher keeping abreast of the times, or to the student beginning an orientation to Wright. This kind of reader is indeed being addressed in these discussions with new and traditional theoretical insights by a group of today's literary critics and scholars responding to one of American literature's most classic and controversial writers.

What defines "classic" and "controversial" under these circumstances? In this collection's review of Wright and his works, one essential point of reference is that readers are making contact with a writer whose seminal works are compass points in the literature of an American culture still defining itself. This process provides excitement and challenge from many vantage points because, like the very best writers in this culture, Wright stimulates us to think about an American experience in deeper and more human terms.

The depth and humanity of Wright's literary contributions are found in structures that intrigued him from nearly the beginning of his development as both a person and a writer. The family unit, the character of religious piety, the prescribed social order, and the way in which a literary artist thinks about depicting his subjects are all enormously important subjects for Wright and for his protagonists as well. These concerns inform all of his writing, and they help to explain Wright's attitude, usually rebellious, toward reality. Wright assaults the formlessness of time and space because he refuses to accept the assumption that his experiences as a black did not figure substantially into the human time and space he occupied.

For instance, if the perceptions we now have about human welfare include a sharper and more sensitive view of the abuse of women and children, we owe some of that gain in perspective to what Wright said to us in *Uncle Tom's Children*. If we are more convinced about an American reality that looks more culturally complex—and in fact always has been with the historical beginnings in the presence of Spaniards, Africans, Europeans and Native Americans—Wright helped cultivate that awareness. Furthermore, Wright's calls for heightened social consciousness simply do not leave readers neutral—either about him as a writer, the different stories which call for it, or the quality of social sensitivity called for. *Native Son*, with its agonizing manchild characterization of Bigger Thomas as both oppressed and oppressor, bears the epic burden of a whole society living out, in flesh and blood, its ambivalence between ideal commitments to justice and equality with its everyday lens on the fluctuations of commerce. And if indeed we are more socially sensitive about our obligations to one another, Wright certainly aided our development.

Yet Wright's assaults are not flawless constructions by any means. The poet-novelist Margaret Walker Alexander recently pointed out that the longer a woman character remains in Wright's stories, the more likely she is to suffer.[1] Mary and Bessie are murdered in *Native Son*, Dot of *The Outsider* is tortured, and Sarah is raped in "Long Black Song." Women as humans do not benefit from Wright's considerable skills and passions, any more than they do in the literature produced by most of Wright's male peers—Hemingway and Faulkner, O'Neill, Cummings, or Wolfe.

James Baldwin early signalled a problem for Wright's audience by challenging Wright's portrayals of the black community.[2] Baldwin saw something very mechanical in Wright's depictions of the black community, something untrue about the wooden responses to death, and religion and family, a triptych of concerns that were, in fact, to make Baldwin famous. The problem, as Baldwin saw it, was the lack of human development cast in its own cultural history—in other words, the orientation of American black people to their living historical circumstances. Baldwin was to become famous for insisting that being poor, especially being poor and black, did not place one outside of human development, particularly as it was defined by Christian piety. Black Americans had, after all, a moral life, like their white counterparts. Baldwin was troubled by not seeing that distinction rigorously demonstrated in Wright. Similarly "In Remembering Richard Wright," Ralph Ellison gracefully discusses the importance of geography, of place, in relationship to the fate of Afro-Americans and to Richard Wright in particular.[3] The issue a reader faces in Ellison's reminiscence, like Baldwin's critique, is to remember not only Wright's work as documentation of the complex nature of the Afro-American as an involuntary yet total player in the American experiment but Wright's compelling and necessary presence as an artist who makes it necessary for other artists to measure some part of themselves against him.

Certainly now the climate could not be more advantageous for an examination of an established writer—and an established black, male writer at that. The canon of American writing has been irreversibly altered by the presence of black women writers in America. The force of their writing shakes the foundation of any permanent thoughts of the classic American writer that excludes women and non-whites. This collection offers an opportunity to fashion a perspective on a literary fixture like Wright by using the signs of our times to sharpen and clarify the space occupied by a major writer in the developing cultural experience of American life.

When Wright turns to the South and the North for autobiographical and fictional presentations, it is not a matter of his readers never having been there before, nor is it a matter of seeing these areas of American life through a particular artistic use of those spaces. Wright illuminates the American experience through the terrain carved out by African

American culture, focusing for the most part on its least privileged members with the tools of literary realism. The path Wright took had always been there. His work, however, altered the texture of the road. Sometimes he widened it, but most often he made us see how rough it was for many to feel positive about their experiences in continental America. There were always real and imaginary rivers to cross in order to gain freedom for blacks and sensitive whites in America, but to get to these streams one had to climb the social Mt. Everest of racism and sexism.

Wright's work has always generated debate. His characterizations and narratives constantly unsettle those seeking symmetrical cause-and-effect relations of persons to the social order where he, Wright, saw none. Even where his symbols of social tyranny (the law, for example) have been challenged by those wishing for less controversial or more precise signs of social oppression, Wright stood steadfastly by the literary and expository forms he used to mirror his view of human experience.

The title for this volume of symposium essays directs attention to the aesthetic complexity inherent in Wright's narratives. The *myths* and *realities* are conceptual instruments for speaking both generally and specifically about Wright's narrative constructs and human passions. Whether he adequately portrayed men and women, children and society, in acceptable ways very often has to do with the angle of vision we have as readers. Our perception, or the process of perceiving, does influence our appreciation of him. His resonating, dramatic "voice"— of text speaking into the attentive ear of the reader—is at the center of these essays on Richard Wright who, in the final analysis, is a classic American writer and, in the best sense of the term, a controversial one, too.

Special thanks are due to Kenneth Perrin, president of West Chester University, for his vigorous support of faculty scholarship; to the English Department for sponsoring this annual forum; and to the students of my senior seminar on Richard Wright and the general survey of African American Literature, whose questions and responses affirm literature's capacity to serve as an instrument for humanizing us all, by reconciling black and white images on and off the printed page.

CHRONOLOGY

1908   Born Richard Nathanael Wright, first son of Nathan and Ella on September 4, near Natchez, Mississippi.

1933   Joins the Chicago John Reed Club and the Communist Party.

1934   His first publications are two poems, "Rest for the Weary" and "A Red Love Note."

1935   The publication of his first piece of journalism, "Joe Louis Uncovers Dynamite."

1938   First of the stories from *Uncle Tom's Children* published.

1940   *Native Son* published.

1941   *Native Son* dramatized on Broadway, produced by John Houseman and directed by Orson Wells. *Twelve Million Black Voices* published.

1945   *Black Boy* published.

1947   The Wrights sail for France and make it their permanent home.

1953   *The Outsider* is published.

1957   *Pagan Spain* and *White Man Listen* are published.

1958   *The Long Dream* is published.

1960   Wright dies. *Eight Men* (1961), *Lawd Today* (1963), and *American Hunger* (1977) published posthumously.[4]

Notes

1. These remarks were made by Dr. Walker Alexander at the National Black Writers Conference on March 25, 1988, held at Medgar Evers College, New York City.

2. James Baldwin, "Alas, Poor Richard," in *Nobody Knows My Name: More Notes of a Native Son* (New York: Dell, 1961), 144–170.

3. Ralph Ellison, "Remembering Richard Wright," in *Going to the Territory* (New York: Random House, 1986), 198–216.

4. Ellen Wright and Michel Fabre, eds., *Richard Wright Reader* (New York: Harper and Row, 1978).

Richard Wright

Artistic Integration of Ideology and Symbolism in Richard Wright's "Fire and Cloud"

Robbie Jean Walker

Contemporary reassessments of Richard Wright's fiction parallel James Weldon Johnson's tribute to the black and unknown bards who "sang far better than they knew." Wright's literary talent was indeed grossly underestimated by many of his own contemporaries. At one time viewed primarily as a strident propagandist when propaganda was the rather curious designation for black fiction that dared to address social and political concerns, Wright is now ranked among the leading literary artists of this century. His reputation as a balanced artist seems finally, albeit belatedly, intact. Were we to concede that Wright's works were ideological pronouncements only, his writings would still deserve a prominent place in the canon of American letters. He did indeed speak to issues that forced Americans to confront the reality of social and political contradictions in a country committed, in theory, to justice and social equality. To limit his contributions to ideology, however, would be tantamount to distortion, for his ideology was often couched in carefully wrought and compelling aesthetic form. Such was his achievement in "Fire and Cloud," a work in which his use of Biblical imagery dramatized at least one dimension of his evolving ideology at a particular time in history.

The symbolic potential of the narrative is evident in the title "Fire and Cloud," which immediately brings to mind the Israelites' triumphant escape from Egyptian bondage. Blacks have traditionally invoked the precedent of God's providential deliverance of the Israelites as a source of hope that the same benevolence would be accorded blacks and ultimately effectuate their own deliverance from racial oppression.

3

What has been described as Wright's uncharacteristic optimism in the resolution of the conflict in this narrative is consistent with the symbolic import of the pillar of a cloud by day and the pillar of fire by night, miraculous agents that shielded the Israelites during their escape from Egyptian bondage. An integral part of the Biblical symbolism, however, does not appear in the title—the dry ground that provided the passage of escape when the waters of the Red Sea were parted. Nonetheless, the dust image, suggestive of the archetypal journey motif, unifies the pivotal decisions made by the protagonist.

In "Fire and Cloud" Wright dramatizes the transformation of the Reverend Daniel Taylor. Initially, the black minister is simply a pawn in the hands of the mayor and other city officials of the small southern town in which he lives, but he emerges as a bona fide leader willing to incur the wrath of all these officials in order to achieve dignity for the people he purports to serve. His transformation has been likened to a baptism, an apt characterization that comports well with Wright's Biblical imagery. Wright's decision to use Biblical imagery derived from his desire to see "things come into Negro life, dressed in Negro clothes, speaking Negro language. . . ." Ellen Wright and Michel Fabre report that Wright communicated these intentions in a June 1936 discussion explaining the genesis of *Uncle Tom's Children*, a collection of four novellas published in 1938. Wright further explained:

> I was drawn to the "Old Negro," the Negro close to the soil, the Negro whose staunch will four centuries of arduous oppression has not broken.   And especially was I drawn toward the religious expression of the "Old Negro." And I made the startling discovery—no doubt a naive one, but after all it was mine, a Negro's—that the images, symbols and attitudes of Christianity were the highest crystallizations of the Negro's will to live he has made in this country. . . (Wright and Fabre 287)

"Fire and Cloud" is the last of four novellas in *Uncle Tom's Children*. Arna Bontemps, in a 1964 symposium honoring Negro writers in the United States, offered the following description of *Uncle Tom's Children*:

> It was drawn from memories of his Mississippi boyhood.   The stories were almost unbearable evocations of cruel realities

which the nation and world had, in the past, been unable or unwilling to face. His purpose, his determination as a prose writer, was to force open closed eyes, to compel America to look at what it had done to the black peasantry in which it was born. (qtd. in Gibson 63)

"Fire and Cloud," winner of several awards as a separate story, has been applauded as a work that strikes a "balance between ideology and symbolic pattern . . . message and medium" (Wright and Fabre 288). Although this view of Wright's artistic achievement in "Fire and Cloud" is not unanimous, his effective integration of symbolism and ideology renders even more meaningless the artificial dichotomy between propaganda and art.

The narrative lends itself well to an analytical model proposed by Roland Barthes in "An Introduction to the Structural Analysis of Narrative." Barthes differentiates between consecutive and consequential functions in narrative, using the latter functions to describe units of meaning that have consequentiality for the continuation of the story. Consecutive functions, on the other hand, may have implications for the continuity of the discourse, but they are not necessarily crucial to the meaning of the narrative itself. These two types of functions parallel the rhetorical considerations of syntagmatic and paradigmatic analysis, the former referring to the linear progression of the discourse and the latter to the more pervasive structural pattern of the work.

Throughout the narrative, the earth image (dust and its variants), the fire image, and the cloud image are prominent, each making its unique contribution to either the consecutive or consequential units of the story. The dust image is more closely associated with the linear or consecutive functions, attaching itself to the forward movement of the story and shifting its symbolic implications as the narrative progresses. Dust, in "Fire and Cloud," almost plays out its full symbolic potential, symbolizing initially human frailty or ultimate nothingness. On yet another level, dust symbolizes the ancient ceremonial acts of casting dust into the air or shaking the dust off one's feet, both acts indicative of an intuitive recognition that further negotiations will be unproductive. The dust image also focuses attention on the earth and is consistent with Wright's effort to illustrate the Negro's call "to do class battle with the only spiritual weapon he has, a belief in his right to the earth" (Wright and Fabre 288). The fire and cloud images, on the other hand, are more atmospheric and pervasive, fulfilling consequential rather than consecutive functions. The symbols associated with the consequential functions are more diffuse in that they impact more profoundly on the atmosphere than on the progression of the narrative. In essence, Wright uses the symbols of the title to illuminate the emotional and political milieu in which the events unfold, thereby dramatizing the emotional turbulence of the protagonist as he searches for strategies to address the prevailing realities. The psychological turbulence is ultimately the catalyst for the pivotal decisions made by the protagonist.

Consequential units of a narrative, according to Barthes' model, either initiate or resolve uncertainties. The uncertainties of the narrative under consideration revolve around the pivotal decisions made by Taylor, the protagonist. The first unit of consequentiality begins with a dejected Taylor walking home from the relief office, having been informed that the reactivation of relief funds to alleviate the hunger of his parishioners was not forthcoming. He cannot erase from his mind the insensitive response of the relief officer: "I'm sorry, Taylor. You'll just have to do the best you can. Explain it to them, make them understand that we cant do anything. . . . Tell them they'll just have to wait" (130). The dramatic tension evident here contributes to the consequentiality of the unit. For Taylor must again face the people in whose behalf he had made the appeal for assistance. And he must face them fully aware of the finality of the relief officer's statement and equally aware of the hopelessness his report would engender.

The tension builds when his son Jimmy rushes to meet him, identifying the three groups of people who are waiting to meet with him. Taylor's apprehension heightens as he contemplates the diverse agendas of the three groups. The church membership is there, expecting his strength in helping them obtain relief from their hunger; the Communist representatives dispatched to the area to organize demonstrations are there, expecting more straightforward, public participation from him; the city officials are there, expecting the acquiescence to which they have become accustomed. Taylor's pattern of response to the conflicting agendas of these groups represents the primary complication and thrust of the narrative. The uncertainty of the first consequential unit is resolved when a surprisingly resolute Taylor tells the city officials that he will not attempt to dissuade his people from participating in the demonstration planned for the following day.

The dust image begins and closes this unit. When Taylor leaves the relief office, he walks home along the dusty road. The dust image permeates this passage and at this level seems to project the notion of human frailty, or ultimate nothingness. This connotation is consistent with Taylor's feeling of desolation—having failed when he wanted so desperately to succeed. The dust image, particularly prominent here, is placed in juxtaposition with the image of the "earth cracking and breaking open, black rich and damp," as Taylor's mind goes back to the times when productivity characterized the land that now lay untilled (132). On his walk home, a car speeding by lifts a great cloud of yellow-brown dust, a symbol that has its correlate in the cloud of dust raised by the car carrying the irate police officer, city commissioner, and baffled mayor away from Taylor's house—the negative moods engendered by their surprise and anger that Taylor has refused to cooperate with their efforts to avert black participation in the demonstration scheduled for the following day.

According to Barthes, symbolic correlates interspersed throughout a narrative contribute significantly to the consequentiality of a unit. The system of correlates, Barthes explains, includes words, symbols, or extended passages that possess seedlike qualities with correlates elsewhere in the narrative either on the same level or a higher level of meaning (Barthes 244). In the former instance, the yellow-brown cloud of dust symbolizes the passion of a dilemma, anxiety added to the initial feeling of defeat. But the second cloud of dust is more symbolic of the alienation felt by the mayor and his group who now view as unproductive any further negotiations with one whom they had previously perceived to be a faithful ally. Thus, the dust image contributes to the progression of the text and has correlates on different levels of meaning.

The fire image in this unit is essentially an embryonic symbol presented as variants of fire or colors associated with fire. On his way home from the meeting, Taylor observes the "green fields" tumbling "to a red sky" (131), and as he envisions what his talk with the city officials will be like, his mind's eye can see the "cigar glowing red" in the mayor's mouth—the color red carrying its usually high association with fire (133). What he envisions becomes reality as the tension mounts during his discussion with the city officials. Disturbed by Taylor's insistence that he will not order the people to refrain from marching the next day, the city officials are angered, and the symbolic implications hinge, at least partially, on the associative symbolism of the color red. Other suggestive images that foreshadow the presentation of the fire image are the sound of the striking match and the angry hiss of the stem as one of the city officials tosses it angrily into a brass spittoon. The fire image, though more suggestive than real in this unit, rather effectively foreshadows the potentially volatile atmosphere in which Taylor must conduct his affairs.

Like the fire image, the cloud image in this unit is most frequently presented as variants of clouds, namely, haze, mist and fog. Taylor posits a metaphorical likeness of the black condition to "one big white fog," and notes "hazy buildings and buildings sprawling mistily" (130). These symbols combine to suggest the clouded vision that frequently characterizes blacks in many dimensions of their struggle. Just as the buildings appear hazy to Taylor and he sees them through something tantamount to a mist, so often does the agenda of blacks fail to clarify, in unambiguous and precise terms, the goals and emphases of the race.

The second consequential unit begins with Jimmy bringing the message to his father that some white men in a car in front of their home want to see him. This segment recounts the beating and humiliation of Taylor by this unidentified mob. Although Taylor has made no concrete promises to the Communist representatives, the power structure is incensed by his refusal to yield to their wishes. The abduction and subsequent torture are designed to teach him a lesson. Blindfolded during the ride from his home to the scene of the torture, Taylor is beaten and mocked by his tormentors and left to stumble home alone during the early morning hours. The unit ends with Taylor's realization that his primary responsibility is to his people. Recalling the deals he has made with the whites in the past and recognizing now the error of his ways, he explains this illumination to Jimmy:

> Ah been wrong erbout a lotta things Ah tol yuh, son. Ah tol
> yuh them things cause Ah thought they wuz right. Ah tol yuh t
> work hard n climb t the top. Ah tol yuh folks would lissen t
> yuh then. But they wont, son! All the will, all the strength,
> all the power, all the numbahs is in the people! (172)

Taylor's construction of reality at this time is both revelatory and tragic. As one reviewer of *Uncle Tom's Children* aptly noted in 1938, ". . . the black man's lot becomes tragic in proportion to his comprehension of his weakness and hopelessness in the world as it is" ("Vigorous Stories" 3).

Thus, the uncertainty initiated when the strange men summon Taylor to the front of his home is now resolved in his determination to make no more deals with whites that will affect the destiny of his people. Moreover, the myopia clouding his vision has been replaced by clarity of vision. And he knows now that he will march with his people if they are still so inclined.

He goes before them and makes a passionate confession.

> Yuh been wonderin how come Ah didnt tell yuh whut
> yuh oughta do. Waal. . . .
>   Sistahs n Brothers, the reason Ah didnt say nothin is cause
> ah didnt know *whut* (italics in original) t say. N the only
> reason Ahm speaking now is cause Ah *do* [italics in original]
> know.
> Ah know whut t do. (177)

This transformation, according to Michel Fabre's assessment in *The Unfinished Quest of Richard Wright*, is reflective of one dimension of Wright's ideological stance at the time. Fabre relates Taylor's symbolic baptism to Wright's political position in relation to the relative merits of individual resistance and collective resistance:

> Taylor's physical ordeal, a symbolic baptism in fire and blood
> when the whites beat him in the woods to intimidate him,
> translates to a higher plane of strength and wisdom. He
> opposes his faith in the solidarity of the masses to the concept
> of personal revenge advocated by his son Jimmy, a typical
> young, individualistic militant. Taylor thereby achieves a
> union of the oppressed, both black and white, whose number
> assures the success of the demonstration. (Fabre 160)

The dust image undergoes variations in this unit that begins with the abduction. Taylor goes to the car to meet the unidentified men, is abducted, blindfolded, driven to an unknown spot, and beaten unmercifully. As he is being driven to the scene of torture, he can hear the car "speeding over gravel" and "rubber tires turning over rough ground" (160). The embedded earth symbolism unfolds in this section and though Taylor is blindfolded, the earth image is particularly strong.

In addition to the sounds, he smells the clay dust. The sound of gravel and the rough road combine with the smell of clay dust to form correlates of the dust image in the preceding section and are indicative of progression—the car moving closer to its destination and Taylor's anxiety building to a terrifying level. The vacillating feelings within him have their parallel in the variants of the dust symbol. When he leaves home, the image is of dust resting filmingly on tree leaves. His departure obviously evokes some uncertainty. But the rough ground and the sound of gravel are reflective of the mounting, agitating turbulence within him as he contemplates the intentions of his abductors. They leave him a long distance from home after beating him and mocking him as he prayed. Taylor travels toward his home on "a brown dusty road winding away in the darkness like a twisting ribbon" (165). Suggestive of both uncertainty and myopia, the long, winding and twisting road matches his emotions: the sobering realization that his previous course of action has indeed been shortsighted and the frightening prospect of a protracted and yet undefined journey.

The embryonic fire images of the first segment—the color red, the black cigar burning red, and the match have correlates in this segment depicting the physical and emotional pain of the beaten minister. Riding away from home with his abductors, he smells the "strong scent of a burning cigarette" (160), a foreshadow of the pain that would soon engulf him. Beginning with the "flash of red [that] shot before his eyes" (159) when the beating began, Taylor's pain is described variously: his back becomes "a sheet of living flame" (163), and a sheet of pain stretches all over his body, "leaping, jumping, blazing in his flesh" (164). Here the most active attributes of fire are accorded his pain—attributes that dramatize both the intensity and depth of his physical anguish. So intense is his pain that he imagines it as both within and outside himself, a part of his total environment, declaring that his "back rested on a bed of fire" (165).

This physical pain symbolized by the fire also has psychological or emotional correlates. Upon returning home, Taylor steals softly to his room to avoid, or at least postpone, discussing his recent humiliation with anyone. Here another dimension of pain accrues as he attempts to explain his physical condition to his son who forces his way into the room: "fire seethed not only in Taylor's back, but all over, inside and out. It was the fire of shame" (169). Even his words in the ensuing discussion are compared to "hot lava out of a mountain from deep down" (171). And later as he talks to his son, admonishing him to let nothing come between him and his people, "fire burned him as he talked" (171). He has now come to the realization that both his dignity and the dignity of his people are at stake and, in consequence, is imbued with a passion that burns within him. Later with the dying fire still lingering in his body, his jerking movements are attributed to his "restlessness of mind" (173). The humiliation and pain from the beating have now altered his consciousness and his transformation is essentially complete.

Although Taylor's commitment to join forces with his people appears to be firm, the resolution achieved at this juncture is challenged by one last complication. The final scene could perhaps technically be included in the falling action inasmuch as Taylor's decision to participate in the demonstration is the critical factor in his transformation. But, functionally, this scene qualifies as a consequential unit in that he must again confront the mayor, who makes a last desperate attempt to control the black community by manipulating the minister. As the marching blacks and poor whites approach City Hall, the mayor again solicits Taylor's cooperation in intimidating the blacks by telling them not to make trouble. Taylor, who has yielded to many such appeals in the past, refuses this time to compromise the principles of his people. Only then is the uncertainty resolved, for Taylor's actions in this instance cannot be taken for granted. The relevant history precludes complete confidence in his ability to withstand the mayor's pleas and empty promises and affords no optimistic predictions of courage.

The resolution of the conflict in "Fire and Cloud" has been persistently problematic for critics concerned about the compromised plausibility and contrived ending. James Young, placing this work in the proletarian tradition, laments that ". . . as so often occurs in proletarian fiction, he [Taylor] leads an all-too-successful march of poor blacks and poor whites who triumphantly gain their demands. And Dan Taylor, now finally enlightened like so many other proletarian heroes during the 1930s proclaims "Freedom belongs to the strong!" (Young 230). Young's dissatisfaction with the pat resolution is shared by Charles T. Davis, who admits that "Fire and Cloud" suffers less from political distortion than does "Bright and Morning Star." Davis attributes this reduced distortion to "Wright's efforts to reconcile Reverend Taylor's Christian principles with the demands for a more

militant resistance to entrenched white injustice"(277). Yet he finds
some features of the narrative problematic.

> We are amazed still that within the space of a few pages the
> Black minister can be exposed both to the scourge of the
> wicked and the temptation of the mighty (that is to say, a
> beating by the town rowdies and a visit from the mayor),and we
> suspect that Taylor's commitment to march with the workers
> excludes more likely alternatives. His decision seems to be
> something less than inevitable. (Davis 277)

While some of these objections are valid ones, Fabre's claim that "the
consistent Biblical symbolism in the hero's character enables the moral
of his maturation to satisfy the law of aesthetics" seems to account
more satisfactorily for the optimistic resolution of the conflict (Fabre
31).

The nature of the ending, the perfect resolution so to speak, is
indeed consistent with the Biblical allusion upon which the narrative is
based. Despite Taylor's broad generalization, "Freedom belongs t' the
strong!," the ending seems to typify only a single victory, not a
permanent and definitive resolution of the entire race struggle. The
victory attained by Taylor and the marchers would, as had its
antecedents, be challenged repeatedly. But the victory is "context-
complete"; the choices made by the protagonist have been sufficiently
appropriate and effective to yield the desired benefits. Wright's belief, at
this time, still included hope for a resolution of America's racial
problems. And idealism is compatible with hope. As late as 1940
when responding to David Cohn's review of *Native Son*,Wright asserted
his continuing belief in the possibility of a solution to racial strife in
America. He wrote to Cohn: "The Negro problem in America is not
beyond solution (I write from a country—Mexico—where people of all
races and colors live in harmony without racial prejudice . . . always
resisting the attempts of Anglo-Saxon tourists and industrialists to
introduce racial hate and discrimination)" (Wright and Fabre 62).

What is so commonly condemned as an overly idealistic and
contrived ending should be viewed in relation to the yet-evolving
ideology of the author and the Biblical symbolism. Evocative of its
Biblical antecedent, the symbolic baptism and deliverance may fall short
of standard requirements of believability or, perhaps more accurately,
plausibility. What the ending does represent, it seems, is a

possibility—an idealized solution to a problem that Wright still believed had a solution. Wright had explained earlier that "Fire and Cloud" represented an effort on his part "to depict in dramatic fashion the relationship between the leaders of both races" (Fabre 135). Implicit here is Wright's belief in the potential of effective leadership in effectuating social and political change. And the miraculous connotation of the title is suggestive of a resolution that may not at all represent, on Wright's part, an attempt to portray southern reality, but to explore possibilities for the solution of a continuing and nationally debilitating social problem.

When Taylor actually joins the march, the full symbolic implications of the title are realized. He looks ahead of him and sees a throng of black and white marchers; he sees the same thing when he looks behind him. Thus, his sense of community is actualized and he lives out the ideal pattern that he had earlier set before Jimmy. "Wes gotta think erbout the people. . . . Whut they suffer is whut ah suffered las night when they whipped me. Wes gotta keep the people wid us" (172). The crowd before him and after him in the line of march sang in unison:

> So the sign of the fire by night
> 'N the sign of the cloud by day
> a-hoverin oer
> jus befo
> As we journey an our way. (178)

Wright's ideological view, at the time, that significant advances in race relations could be attained only through collective resistance is appropriately dramatized through images compatible with deliverance. Now that the people are with Taylor and he with the people, a "collective wherewithal" emerges that provides the courage to pursue deliverance vigorously. The protection symbolized by the pillar of a cloud and pillar of fire is actualized through the resistance of the marching throng and the corresponding knowledge that the mayor cannot harm them because they are sufficiently strong in numbers to withstand his threats. The symbolic antecedents achieve full potential when the crowd "parts" to allow the mayor to approach Taylor, the minister having refused the mayor's orders to come to the front of the line. The shifting symbolism throughout the narrative is particularly suggestive of the uneven and frequently faltering efforts that have characterized the race struggle. And the long winding road, a familiar metaphor in black literature, is at once reminiscent of the numerous reversals attributable to ambiguous agendas *and* the long, arduous journey that social and political transition requires.

References

Barthes, Roland. "An Introduction to the Structural Analysis of Narrative." *New Literary History*, 72 (1975): 237–272.

Davis, Charles T., *Black Is the Color of the Cosmos*. Ed. Henry Louis Gates, Jr. New York: Garland, 1982.

Fabre, Michel, *The Unfinished Quest of Richard Wright*. Trans. Isabel Barzun. New York: William Morrow & Co., 1973.

Gibson, Donald. *Five Black Writers*. New York: New York University Press, 1970.

"Vigorous Stories Portray Tragedy of Southern Negro. Negro Writer's Painfully Authentic Sketches Carry Powerful Indignation at Oppression." Rev. of *Uncle Tom's Children* in *Dallas Morning News*, 27 March 1938, sec. 3:10. Rpt. in *Richard Wright: The Critical Reception*. Ed. John M. Reilly. New York: Burt Franklin & Co., 1978.

Wright, Ellen, and Michel Fabre, eds. *Richard Wright Reader*. New York: Harper and Row, 1978

Wright, Richard. *Uncle Tom's Children*. New York: Harper and Row, 1938.

Young, James O. *Black Writers of the Thirties*. Baton Rouge: Louisiana State University Press, 1973.

Black Orpheus Refused:
A Study of Richard Wright's
The Man Who Lived Underground

Stephen Soitos

Through me is the way into the woeful city
Through me is the way into eternal woe
Through me is the way among the lost people.

(words over the gate of hell)
Dante

One would tap the brain for any knowledge of initiation rites lying dormant there, recognizing that life depended on it, that initiation was the beginning of transformation and that the ecology of the self, the tribe, the species, the earth depended on just that.

The Salt Eaters
Toni Cade Bambara

Richard Wright's *The Man Who Lived Underground* can best be interpreted as a synthesis of Eurocentric myth and Afro-American sensibilities. The isolation of the character, his namelessness through most of the narrative, and his lack of a developed, personalized past suggests the classical mythical hero. Furthermore, Wright places his character in an underground world, which is a classic mythical testing ground for a hero in pursuit of higher personal and cultural knowledge. As in his earlier novel *Native Son* the psychological transformation of the main character comes through violence, both imagistic and active. But *The Man Who Lived Underground* does more than reflect Eurocentric mythic conventions. It uses Eurocentric myth in a new way, so that Wright does not just uncritically imitate patterns in this novel. Instead he reworks ancient mythic structure into a new context of Afro-American experience. In effect Wright deconstructs Euro-myth and reconstructs it in an Afro-centric way. I suggest that the novel illustrates the descent motif in peculiarly personal colors, making important critical points about modern American society and its exclusion of black Americans.

Wright's single-character, powerful, short narrative is about a man who descends into a sewer in flight from the police and lives under a nameless city suffering the horrors of a modern hell until resurfacing leads to rejection and entombment in the sewer he tries to escape. Richard Wright "once described fiction as the exploration of an idea, and to a great extent his novels and stories reflect his intellectual concerns" (Hamalian and Volpe 673). The idea behind *The Man Who Lived Underground* owes less influence to existentialism as some critics such as Edward Margolies suggest, than to a modern re-working of the Greek myth of Orpheus.

The Orpheus myth is primarily a story of descent and return. Orpheus is married to Eurydice. When she dies he follows her to the underworld hoping to free her and influence Hades, god of the underworld, with his music. Orpheus triumphs over obstacles and trials in the underworld and is granted his wish, under the condition that he not look backwards before he and Eurydice are above ground. At the edge of Hades, Orpheus makes the mistake of turning to look for Eurydice while he is in the light and she is still in the shadow. Eurydice is returned to the underground and Orpheus goes on to preach a new religion urging a turn from Dionysian frenzy to one of devotion to Apollo, god of reason. Dionysus wreaks revenge by having his maenads kill Orpheus while he is in his temple.

The Orpheus myth is only one example of many myths that share similar characteristics and are defined by Joseph Campbell in his book *Hero with a Thousand Faces* as a monomyth:

> The standard path of the mythological adventure of the hero is a magnification of the formula represented in the rites of passage: separation—initiation—return, which might be named the nuclear unit of the monomyth. A hero ventures forth from the world of common day into a region of supernatural wonder: fabulous forces are there encountered and a decisive victory is

> won: the hero comes back from this mysterious adventure with
> the power to bestow boons on his fellow man. (Campbell 30)

This monomyth is the most common of culturally shared
mythological formulas, but we understand this journey also as a
symbolic one that represents a descent into the unconscious in both an
individual and collective sense:

> "The transcendent function," Jung called it. This ability to
> make the transition between the conscious and unconscious (to
> descend to Hades and yet to return to the upper world) and yet
> never annihilate the conscious. Orpheus is that transcendent
> function . . . the daring to confront *all* of the psyche and not be
> overwhelmed by the daring. (Hughes 112)

Fred Daniels' story of descent differs somewhat from the traditional
hero's quest. Daniels does not choose (by answer to a call or by his own
free will to attain a goal) to descend into the underworld. He is pursued
and forced down. "I've got to hide, he told himself," is the very first
sentence of the novel. From that moment on the novel is one long
attempt to escape not only a crime he didn't commit but also a cruel,
violent culture that infuses Daniels' being with a primal angst based on
unearned guilt.

Essentially, all we know about Daniels is that he is accused falsely
of the murder of a Mrs. Peabody. Daniels professes his innocence more
than once in the novel, and in the end we know from outside
confirmation that he is innocent. But is his innocence enough to save
him? Wright's answer is no, because Daniels' innocence is not
supported by a forgiving, life-affirming world. The culture Daniels is
born into is unjust, greedy and violent. This is demonstrated in an
important way by the fact that Daniels is accused and beaten and made
to sign a false confession because he is black.

Daniels' hiding place is a sewer because it's the safest place to
escape the police. But his entrance into the underground soon leads to
transformation and revelation. Every underground hell has a river Styx
and in Fred Daniels' case the river comes for him ". . . a gray spout of
sewer water jutted up from the underground and lifted the circular metal
cover, juggled if for a moment, then let it fall with clang." Daniels
descends into the manhole and ". . . was washed violently into an ocean
of warm, leaping water." He is sealed off from above by a policeman

who puts the cover back. "Looming above his head in the rain a white face hovered over the hole." Thereafter the novel is populated by a series of disembodied, hateful white faces representing an oppressive culture Daniels can neither escape nor come to terms with.

Daniels' journey into darkness begins with his confrontation with a snarling rat, which corresponds to Cerberus, who guards the gates of hell. Passing beyond the rat, which he beats off with a metal pole, Daniels descends deeper into darkness until he reaches a cave. The labyrinthian course is one leading from "watery darkness" into a "hole with walls of damp earth leading into blackness." Daniels eventually lives in this cavern like a hunted animal, and in the process of exploring the boundaries of the underground world he must negotiate a series of dream-like trials of initiation.

> Once having traversed the threshold, the hero moves in a dream landscape of curiously fluid, ambiguous forms, where he must survive a succession of trials. (Campbell 30)

He first witnesses a black church service through a hole in a wall. His first impulse is to laugh because he rejects this black representation of organized religion and community, although by the end of the novel he achieves a personal spirituality that manifests itself in part by his singing a hymn he hears in this church. "The singing swept on and he shook his head disagreeing in spite of himself." Throughout the novel Daniels is isolated from any concept of community. In his worst moments of terror Daniels reaches out to no one, neither god, man, woman, or a group. His isolation is complete. Only in one brief moment of recollection does he even mention that he is married. The only thing that indentifies him is his color, and he himself never mentions it. But the culture he lives in dehumanizes him by using his color against him, and because he is defined by color in this way the reader begins to understand that Wright has written an Afro-American novel of bitter insight about a trapped Afro-American male.

Part of Daniels' tragedy as an Afro-American is that he is isolated from shared behavior like no other hero of myth. In the traditional role of the descent hero, the trial is undergone for the benefit of the community or in the service of others, as Orpheus does in trying to save Eurydice from death. Daniels lacks this commitment to partner or community. He differs also from the traditional hero in that he lacks the aid of a supernatural force usually manifested by a helpful crone or a fairy godmother.

> What such a figure represents is the benign, protected power of destiny . . . a promise that the peace of paradise, which was known first within the mother's womb, is not to be lost; that it supports the present and stands in the future as well as in the past. (Campbell 72)

Daniels is given no assurance of the continuity of the life force at any point in his long journey. His rejection of the black church group and his steadfast internalization of conflict emphasizes his totally divorced condition. This is important to the overall alienation theme of the novel. This alienation leads to a spiritual enlightenment that for all its idiosyncratic qualities has universal meaning. In the end Daniels is rejected by both black and white communities, but his spiritual message is still a valid one.

Immediately after parting from the church service Daniels loses track of time and confronts the first of many death images—the nude dead baby caught in sewer debris. Certainly the underworld is a place of death, but Daniels' hell is visited by truly horrible manifestations of death without any hope of rebirth or renewal. Each minor triumph of Daniels, rather than leading him towards a renewed sense of self or towards completion and ascent, fixes him inexorably deeper into defeat and death.

If we look at the underground world as a symbolic journey to the source of the psyche (individual and collective), a journey leading ultimately towards revelation and rebirth, then this symbol of infant death suggests little hope for regeneration in the world as it is. An infant should be the symbol of hope, but what Daniels confronts in this discarded child is the inexpressible horror, not just of death, but of the death of possibility: "The eyes were closed . . . the fists clenched, as though in protest, and the mouth gaped black in a soundless cry." The natal core of American culture is frozen in death. "He straightened and drew in his breath feeling that he had been staring for all eternity at the nipples of veined water skimming impersonally over the shriveled limbs. He felt condemned as when the policeman had accused him."

Daniels pushes the baby back into the sewer water and in further exploration breaks through an underground wall and sees "The nude, waxen figure of a man stretched out upon a white table." Next to the man is a coffin and a vial of embalming fluid with which undertakers are replacing the dead man's blood. Daniels is surrounded by images of brutal, uncaring death at both ends of the spectrum of existence. Further on he comes to the movie theatre, and Daniels reacts as he had with the church people. He laughs disdainfully at the absurdity of these people's delusions. Daniels has begun to strip away the fantasies that make life tolerable, and underneath he finds not health and growth, but rot and death. "These people were laughing at their lives, he thought with amazement. They were shouting and yelling at the animated shadows of themselves . . . he could awaken them . . . these people were children, sleeping in their living, awake in their dying."

Daniels retreats to his cave after finding food and tools. The cave increasingly becomes the center of his existence underground, and it takes on aspects of mother womb, cell and grave. He falls asleep and has a dream about being swept out to sea. In the dream he tries to save a lady and her child who are drowning. He dives down into the water to save the woman and in the process loses both woman and child. The psychological reading of the anima figure is quite clear. As with Orpheus and Eurydice and many other descent myths, the hero at some point confronts the feminine principle:

> The meeting with the goddess (who is incarnate in every woman) is the final test of the talent of the hero to win the boon of love (charity: amor fati), which is life itself enjoyed as the encasement of eternity. (Campbell 118)

The mystical union or marriage that this vision represents is not completed, and the implication of the impossibility of a healthy union between male and female in American society is strongly drawn.

After waking from this dream, Daniels digs again. This time he uncovers a room which reveals a safe full of money and jewels. "The white hand went in and out of the safe, taking wads of bills and cylinders of coins." At first he is lured by the money, but he soon finds that wealth isolates him, and the white culture which covets it, from any source of spiritual continuity. Before Daniels can return to record the combination of the safe and break into it, he further explores the basement he is in. He finds a sack, a radio and a frigid meat locker hung with dead animals from which he steals a meat cleaver. He gets into the fruit and meat market, and it is at this mid-point in his journey that he resurfaces from the underground and has to make a decision. It is here that we for the first time learn the bare minimum of facts about his past. "Sprawling before him in his mind was his wife, Mrs. Wooten for whom he worked, the three policemen who picked him up. . . . He possessed them now more completely than he had ever possessed them when he lived above ground. . . . Emotionally he hovered between the world aboveground and the world underground."

This is a crucial point in the novel in relation to the descent theme. For the most important aspect of the journey underground is the return. The risk is monumental, for he who attempts the descent gambles with his life among men because there is always the possibility that the return cannot be completed and the hero will remain underground.

> For it is not enough simply to descend, not in mythic or psychological or aesthetic terms. Odysseus needs to come home. The mind that never returns from the depths of the unconscious is mad. (Hughes 113)

Similarly, Orpheus is a traditional symbol of wholeness that Daniels, if he is to model, must follow to the aboveground and communicate what he has learned on his journey underground.

> Orpheus was ideally suited to bridge the gap between modes of looking at the world. (Strauss 7)

The two modes are Dionysian and Apollonian, representing the unconscious and the conscious, the irrational and the rational. To complete his symbolic quest, Daniels must surface. The episode in the fruit market is his first failure at this. He gains the street but can go no further because of the newspaper with the headline: "HUNT NEGRO FOR MURDER." His immediate reaction is to retreat back into the basement. "They know I didn't do anything, he muttered. But how could he prove it? He had signed a confession. Though innocent he felt guilty, condemned."

Daniels keeps a meat cleaver and returns to the room near the safe and copies the combination. In the process he sees someone stealing money and Daniels reflects that he wanted to steal the money also, but for different reasons. "He [Daniels] wanted to steal the money for the sensation involved in getting it, and he had no intention whatever of spending a penny of it. . . ."

In fact the breaking into the safe and the resultant spree of maniacal energy in which Daniels papers the walls of his cave with money and litters the floor with precious jewels and diamonds can only be seen as a symbolic act, demonstrating for Daniels a most important discovery. "There was in him no sense of possessiveness; he was intrigued with the form and color of money, with the manifold reactions which he knew that men above ground held toward it."

To further prove the point of the meaningless of the money and jewels, Daniels also steals a typewriter in which he had just pecked out his name in lower case and unspaced letters "freddaniels." "He did not feel that he was stealing, for the cleaver, the radio, the money, and the typewriter were all on the same level of value . . . they were the serious toys of the men who lived in the dead world of sunshine and rain he had left, the world that had condemned him, branded him guilty."

Daniels' subterranean quest enters a most crucial phase here in the last half of the novel. As the aboveworld's values are revealed to be corrupt, based on greed and violence, the manifestations of death to the human spirit become manifold. Daniels retreats to his cave where his concept of reality becomes more and more distorted.

He litters his world with the meaningless artifacts of money and violence that are his only birthright in the corrupt white culture. He struggles to create an underground cave of meaning to help orient himself to truer, more substantial values, but a cacophony of bizarre images and increasingly irrational acts plague him. He wires his room for electricity, he fires the watchman's gun, he uses hundred dollar bills as wallpaper, he drapes watches around the cave, he forgets his name and finds his identity dissolving. In the end he can't even remember why he was running from the police.

Now begins his last and most terrifying descent into himself and his culture, searching for the center that can't be found. Disintegration and figurative dismemberment are themes of the descent myth, but successful revelations are predicated on the survival of the hero by a process of reintegration that Daniels can't complete because he is prevented from doing so by the white culture he was born into.

His last and most important revelation comes in a waking dream in which he sees himself floating above the world that is reflected in the glittering diamonds imbedded in the mud floor. "He looked down upon land and sea as men fought, as cities were razed, as planes scattered death upon towns, as long lines of trenches waved and broke." Daniels vision of the apocalypse is consistent with the theme of prophecy and cultural self-destruction in the novel. His quest becomes complete with his final vision of universal death.

He wakes with the knowledge that he must return to the aboveworld to communicate his knowledge of approaching catastrophe. "The spell was broken. He shuddered, feeling that, in spite of his fear, sooner or later he would go up into that dead sunshine and somehow say something to somebody about all this."

> The return and reintegration with society, which is indispensable to the continuous circulation of spiritual energy into the world, and which, from the standpoint of community, is the justification of the long retreat, the hero himself may find the most difficult requirement of all. (Campbell 36)

Before leaving the underground Daniels has two further experiences that support his transformation into a prophet. The first is a dream in which he sees himself dead on a table where he stands to one side protecting himself, " . . . warding off the people." In this dream and in the final dreamlike witness of the watchman killing himself because he's falsely accused of a crime that Daniels has committed, we can symbolically see Daniels killing off his old self to make way for a new being. Out of the old self emerges a new self, but this new Daniels still needs to find a center and a community willing to pay attention to his revelations.

Immediately after witnessing the death of the watchman Daniels breaks into the aboveground.

> The orphic poet seeks to regenerate himself particularly by means of the voyage downward. With its attendant self-recognition through remembrance and its mandatory self-transformation followed by a return to the world that will become the ground of a vaster transformation. (Strauss 12)

What is important to remember here is that Daniels is now a representative of underground knowledge. This type of knowledge is associated with feelings and emotion rather than rational thought. "His mind said no; his body said yes; and his mind couldn't understand his feelings." Hence, Daniels' madness is a prophetic madness—but still a madness—unless he can communicate his vision to aboveground authorities and thereby share the wisdom of descent.

But the representatives of white culture want nothing to do with black Daniels, and neither do his own people. He is first rejected by the black church. They won't let him tell his story and thereby refuse a true spiritual visionary of their own color. His final destination is the police station, and the policemen also see him as a madman or psycho. They try to tell him that he is free and rip up his signed confession, but Daniels is too absorbed with his own vision to understand them. His Dionysian self is in control. "The policeman stood before him demanding logical answers and he could no longer think with his mind; he thought with his feelings and no words came."

Daniels' rationality is enfeebled by the weight of his apocalyptic vision and his desire to communicate the wisdom of new values based not on money or power or violence but on love and pity. As a vehicle to transmit this message Daniels fails because of the intractable evil of the white world, represented by the three policemen.

Although Daniels' personal metamorphosis has been effected and he recognizes a higher moral value in the brotherhood of man, Daniels can only lead the white men to the edge of the underworld; he can't force them to make the journey of revelation that he has made.

> He could barely contain his rising spirits. They would see what he had seen; they would feel that he had felt. He would lead them through all the holes he had dug . . . he wanted to make a hymn, prance about in physical ecstasy, throw his arms about the policemen in fellowship.
>
> He was eager to take them to the cave now. if he could show them what he had seen, then they in turn would show others and those others would feel as they had felt and soon everybody would be governed by the same sense of pity.

In the end, although Wright has downplayed Daniels' blackness, it is Lawson who recognizes the essential reason for Daniels' rejection as a returned prophet. Lawson's reason for Daniels' madness is that: "Maybe it's because he lives in a white world."

The implication that a black man will never be accepted in a white world is an important one coming as it does at the end of the novel. Daniels is a threat to the stability of Lawson's society first and foremost because he is black. Daniels' prophetic "madness" is conclusive evidence that a black man can achieve a human wisdom that white society can't comprehend or incorporate. Therefore, by Lawson's rules it is inevitable that Daniels must be rejected not just as Orpheus, but as *black Orpheus*. Wright has successfully transformed a Eurocentric myth into an important Afro-American statement:

> "What did you shoot him for, Lawson?"
> "I had to."
> "You've got to shoot his kind. They'd wreck things."

Lawson's final statement stands as a prophetic indictment of white American culture which has no place for spiritual understanding and exists not as a society of the brotherhood of man but as a culture that continues to kill off the best of its kind.

References

Campbell, Joseph. *The Hero With a Thousand Faces*. Princeton: Princeton University Press, 1930.

Hamalian, Leo, and Edmond L. Volpe. *Eleven Modern Short Novels*. New York: G. P. Putnam's Sons, 1958.

Hughes, Richard E. *The Lively Image: 4 Myths in Literature*. Cambridge: Winthrop Publishers, Inc., 1958.

Strauss, Walter A. *Descent and Return: The Orphic Theme in Modern Literature*. Cambridge: Harvard University Press, 1971.

Richard Wright and
Afro-American Gothic

Joseph Bodziock

In his book *Singers of Daybreak* Houston Baker noted that white critics have traditionally regarded black American literature as "excessively didactic."[1] Such has often been the fate of Richard Wright's 1940 novel *Native Son*. Leslie Fiedler typified the perspective of white critics when he wrote that he saw Wright as no more than a "belated writer of the Thirties" who wrote novels that were "mere 'protest literature,' incapable of outliving the causes that occasioned his wrath."[2] This is a fate for which Wright himself must bear some responsibility, for *Native Son* is indeed shot through with enough moments of heavy-handed naturalism as to make the novel read like a textbook.

Yet there are odd moments in *Native Son*—moments of gothic splendor we might deem incompatible with the tenets of naturalism. There are ghostly premonitions and apparitions, a curse that will consume the hero, Poe-esque images of conscience and guilt, an impenetrable world of white mystery, and what at times appears to be the free mix of the rational with the supernatural. Even in "How Bigger Was Born," Wright's introduction to the novel in which he incisively analyzes the methodology for creating his protagonist Bigger Thomas, he acknowledges an unusual set of writers as the frame of reference within which we can understand the "naturalism" of *Native Son*:

> But we do have in the Negro the embodiment of a past tragic enough to appease the spiritual hunger of even a James; and we have in the oppression of the Negro a shadow athwart our

national life dense and heavy enough to satisfy even the gloomy broodings of a Hawthorne. And if Poe were alive, he would not have to invent horror; horror would invent him.[3]

These are romanticists, writers less interested in evaluating the intricacies of the social process than in creating a symbolic tapestry that evokes the moral center of the individual. Yet Wright's acknowledgements are quite pertinent, for co-existing with Wright's naturalism—and that naturalism is there—is a gothic mode that endows the naked surface of *Native Son* with a symbolic and moral power.

Dan McCall, who in his book *The Example of Richard Wright* first noted the presence of the gothic in *Native Son*, believed that although he used the trappings of the gothic, Wright could not create a true gothic romance. Unlike Hawthorne or Poe, Wright had "no possibility of settled [historical] distance" between himself and the values intrinsic to the story he was telling. When Wright remarks that horror would invent Poe he is articulating a truism of race relations in America: the horror of racial enmity was active and ongoing, not a static moment in the past waiting to be re-imagined like a still-life portrait. Moreover the "willful distortions" that defined the artistry of a Hawthorne or Poe "were forced upon Wright by the dominant culture." Ultimately the difference between Wright and the romanticists he invoked was that the romanticists "could erect fantasies in the head; Wright was trying to rid himself of the fantasy in his."[4]

But what is the gothic doing in the work of a man devoted to the rational perception of life and social processes? In *White Man, Listen!* (1957) Wright would reject the sort of superstition and fantasy that gave credence to a gothic vision of the world. He condemned the dogmas of ancient religions because of the "emotional dependence they foster" and because they "prevent the masses from moving into the modern world."[5] As Boris Max, a spokesman for the rational in *Native Son* put it more succinctly, "I do not deal in magic."[6] In the end Wright does not betray his rationalist sensibility, because in the final assessment *Native Son* is *not* a gothic romance. But through the first two books of *Native Son*—through our introduction to Bigger Thomas, his employment as a chauffeur with the wealthy Dalton family, his accidental killing of their daughter Mary, his pitiful attempts to hide the crime, and his capture as he lay spread-eagled in the snow—Wright does play with gothic forms, which suggests that he saw a valuable if limited potential in having the aura of gothic romance suffuse his naturalistic testament.

We will examine the gothic in *Native Son* from two perspectives—its European origins, and its transformation in America. Although the European form of the gothic would seem to better suit Wright's ostensible social purposes, if Wright were going to free himself from the fantasy that haunted him, he would have to lift his tale out of the netherworld of proletarian literature and its passion for external and objectifiable processes. The American form of the gothic and its obsession with sin, retribution, and moral order ultimately make the gothic in *Native Son* meaningful. Through the character of Bigger Thomas Wright was able to show the power of the white mythology and its terrible need to sustain its domination.

In its European mode the gothic jibed with Wright's overt naturalistic purposes. As it had been developed in Europe of the eighteenth and nineteenth centuries the gothic tale had an undercurrent of caste consciousness.[7] It became the imaginative battleground where the emergent middle class, celebrating the natural rights of the individual, tilted at a moribund aristocracy. As is typical in this form, the non-aristocratic hero resisted and subverted a decadent aristocracy shielded behind the walls of a crumbling castle, isolated from the modern world. The quasi-supernatural content of the gothic exemplified the haughtiness of the aristocracy, who abided by no rules but their own and whose powers were so deeply entrenched and old that they had become mythic.

The fundamental forms and values of the European gothic, in fact, were commonly incorporated into a most significant earlier body of Afro-American literature—the antebellum slave narratives written during the thirty years prior to the Civil War. Narrators such as Frederick Douglass, Harriet Jacobs, Henry Bibb and Charles Ball knew first hand that the persistence of the slave system depended upon mystery and myth to sustain its ill-gotten power. Douglass, for example, commented on the "Grim, cold, and unapproachable" nature of the Lloyd plantation commanded by a man known only to the child Douglass as the mysterious and quasi-deific Old Master. The plantation was a place devoted to "outward seeming" and the glory of bounty— even wretched excess—in which a privileged slaveholding aristocracy could indulge and from which the slaves were excluded:

> . . . the highly favored inmates of the mansion are literally
> arrayed "in purple and fine linen," and fare sumptuously every
> day!   The table groans under the heavy and blood-bought
> luxuries gathered with pains-taking care, at home and abroad.
> Field, forest, rivers, and seas, are made tributary here. Immense
> wealth, and its lavish expenditure, fill the great house with all
> that can please the eye, or tempt the taste. Here, appetite, not
> food is the great *desideratum.* [8]

Richard Wright the rationalist would have found Douglass's perceptions
most acute and appealing, for Douglass's Lloyd Plantation, like the
white world of *Native Son* as Bigger sees it, was a place where "Reason
is imprisoned . . . and passions run wild." [9]

Bigger Thomas, too, is caught in a circle of desire and frustration;
even before he meets the wealthy Daltons and experiences first-hand the
evidence of fulfilled appetite he is aware of the mystery and the power
of the white world. He is dazzled by its technology and intrigued and
intimidated by what Wright, through Bigger's thoughts, terms the
"ultimate taboo" of robbing a white man. He is titillated by its
cinematic images of white abandon, where power and license
comfortably coexist. At times Bigger seems full of the images of that
world's appetite and the ease with which it seems to fulfill its desires.

He and his friends trade tall tales about whites—specifically
empowered wealthy whites who are emotionally, physically, and
psychologically out of reach. When Bigger sees a campaign poster for
Buckley, he mutters to himself "I bet that sonofabitch rakes off a
million bucks in graft a year. Boy, if I was in his shoes for just one
day I'd *never* have to worry again." [10] His friend Jack tells Bigger "you
ought to take that job [with the Daltons]. You don't know what you
might run into. My ma use to work for rich white folks and you ought
to hear the tales she used to tell." [11] Jack and Bigger tell each other about
licentious and indiscriminate women—just like on the movie screen,
with its larger-than-life images and celebrated performers whose fame
sanctifies the "truth" of what one sees. Jack tells of mattresses stuffed
with money and of butlers who roll their masters over while they sleep.

Thus before Bigger even meets the Daltons he is firmly
indoctrinated into a way of thinking that assigns mythic values to the
white race.   When Bigger does first arrive at the Daltons and meets
with the family, Wright creates a stark contrast between the aspiring
black man and the emblems of white power that ultimately exclude

him. "This was a cold and distant world," Bigger perceives about the white neighborhood where the Daltons lived, "a world of white secrets carefully guarded." The Dalton mansion itself is enclosed by "a high, black, iron picket fence." "All he had felt in the movie was gone," Bigger thinks; "only fear and emptiness filled him now."[12]

Bigger is terrified and disoriented by the symbols and images that greet him in the Dalton mansion. He is aware of them, and they are darkly foreboding, but their significance only scurries at the edge of his consciousness. What comprehensible meanings these symbols and images might have elude Bigger:

> On the smooth walls were several paintings whose nature he tried to make out, but failed. He would have liked to examine them, but he dared not. Then he listened; a faint sound of piano music floated to him from somewhere. He was sitting in a white home; dim lights burned around him; strange objects challenged him; and he was feeling angry and uncomfortable.[13]

In this place even the medium of language itself is a private, excluding code to be deciphered. As Bigger listens to Mr. and Mrs. Dalton talk about him, he could only think that the "long strange words they used made no sense to him; it was another language."[14]

While the Dalton house is a shrine to materialism, the family itself seems not quite of this world. Mr. Dalton first appears to Bigger as a disembodied voice. The blind Mrs. Dalton seems "like a ghost," an ethereal, near-mythic figure whose major purpose in the novel is to serve as allegory for the iconographic power of white women. Mary Dalton, the daughter who will be accidentally smothered by Bigger that night, is described not as the vibrant young girl she is supposed to be but in terms that mark her as a re-animated corpse: "She looked like a doll in a show window: black eyes, white face, red lips."[15] Her garish, unmodulated coloring gives her the look of violent death; and that, in fact, will be hers. If we read Mary as a symbol within the context of the European gothic, then we can perceive her as a symbol of the stagnant present and future awaiting the ruling class. The suggestion of death and morbidity, the chilling image of innocence artificially preserved and static, betrays the "outward seeming" of life.

The gothic conventions, then, have purpose and promise in *Native Son*—Wright does not simply offer a set of supernatural gewgaws but offers gothic imagery within the context of a social clash. When the lawyer Boris Max defends Bigger at his trial in the last section of the book, Max sounds a mild note of triumph when he suggests that the killing of Mary Dalton gave Bigger the chance "to act and to feel that his actions carried weight" (a sentiment echoed by Dan McCall).[16] This would suggest that the promise of the European gothic had been realized in *Native Son*, for the aspiring individual had somehow thrown off the weight of the oppressive white mythos and committed a self-willed and individuated act.

But there are two fundamental problems that make this an unsuitable reading for *Native Son*. First, in the context of race and racial hierarchies the symbolic tapestry and racial power of the Daltons was validated by the body of American whites, not simply by an American white aristocracy. Wright knew that the white masses were not about to yield their domination in favor of a more egalitarian society, much less turn over the responsibility for such a radical change to a black hero (especially in the world of American fiction, where traditionally black heroism, when it even existed, was either mediated by a white hero or a white author). In *Native Son* it is the white masses who act with the least amount of rationality: they punish a multitude of blacks for one man's transgression, they pursue and capture Bigger, and they are the most explicitly virulent about seeing him punished.

Second, the European gothic contains a fundamental message of optimism that would have transformed Bigger at best into a tragic hero and at worst a pathetic victim—thus effectively undercutting the necessary tension of *Native Son*. To follow through with this would mean that Wright failed to generate the dread he so deeply wanted to create in the character of Bigger. Wright sought to forsake the type of black heroic character he had created for his short story collection *Uncle Tom's Children*. For *Native Son* he wanted to elicit fear, not pity, so that through Bigger Thomas he could compel a reader to clearly see the dark and troubling pathology of race relations in America.

Wright shaped Bigger's character in such a way as to forbid any notions of heroism—in a strict romantic sense—from gathering about him. Wright saw to it that no reader mistake Bigger for a redemptive hero sent to overturn a stagnated order. Bigger is sullen and mean-spirited; he is a petty thief and a bully, given to raging at his family and friends and capable of using and humiliating his lover Bessie. When he is overwhelmed by his fear as he flees from those who pursue him for killing Mary Dalton, he is capable of raping and murdering

Bessie. Wright, then, did not want Bigger to be an heroic man whose goodly nature was mistaken or disavowed. Bigger is the sort of black man who rouses fear and loathing in whites and compels them to respond—he is the sort of character that calls the oppressive white mythos out of hiding, so to speak, to reveal itself in all its horrific and mythic glory.

But despite his contrariness, Bigger is no rebel with a cause. A key point to remember here is that Bigger does not reject the mythology of the white world; rather, he consumes it. We have seen the myths upon which he nourished himself earlier. On the surface these myths and images are mocking, but they are deeply tinged with envy. How embarrassed would empowered whites be to know these myths, to know that young black men told each other tales of whites with unbounded appetites, glorious and enviable excess, and unbounded freedom to indulge those appetites? After all, appetite lay at the heart of the American mission to consume a land and a planet. These are tales told by those thirsting after the symbols of power. As he anticipates his job at the Daltons, Bigger, "full of the sense of a life he had never seen," asks Jack "You reckon folks really act like that?" Jack answers simply "Sure, man. They rich."[17] That perhaps is what makes Bigger and his ilk such a threat—not their inclination to violence or their social recalcitrance but their cold-blooded lust for the power.

Bigger, then, was the perfect sort of character to force the white mythos to play its hand, and that is ultimately where the meaningful use of the gothic in *Native Son* lies. If the novel were going to be true to its Americanist title and true to the vicissitudes of race in America, its world of gothic symbols and archetypes needed to do more than resurrect a hoary tale of social upheaval. Wright knew that American racism was neither moribund nor in retreat. But the gothic form, as it had been transformed in America of the eighteenth and nineteenth centuries, allowed Wright to bore into the white American psyche and find the anxieties and terrors that dwelled there. The American gothic replaced the social struggle of the European gothic with a Manichean struggle between the moral forces of personal and community order and the howling wilderness of chaos and moral depravity. Furthermore, the moral chaos could be objectified as a black human being (who eventually displaced the American Indian), whether it be in the benign form of Topsy of *Uncle Tom's Cabin,* or the more malefic forms that appeared in Hawthorne or Poe.

Bigger Thomas was the heir to those characters though Wright used him for a far different purpose. For Wright Bigger was a means to compel the white mythos to act—to reveal itself—not so it could be conquered but so its spiritual ugliness could be comprehended. Because of what Bigger did (and what he was) Bigger in a sense calls forth the white mythos to reveal its naked power for all of Wright's readers to see. Bigger does not will what happens; in fact the white mythos compels Bigger to fulfill its mythic expectations. Bigger is taken on a profound journey through the landscape of gothic nightmare. He sees the white world and its mythic power unleashed and rampant as he had never seen it before. It is a place where Bigger witnesses first hand the mythmaking process that made him what he was and governed what he did.

While a settled distance was not available to Wright, the form of the American gothic could offer a settled perspective—a *persistence* of history, since meaning was measured in moral rather than social terms (a persistence akin to that which possessed many of Hawthorne's characters). Although the problem of Bigger Thomas was set in a palpable context, as James Baldwin observed, the product of Bigger Thomas was simply the increment of an historical process: "In our image of the Negro breathes the past we deny, not dead but living yet and powerful, the beast in our own jungle of statistics."[18]

In America, the black man had entered the American consciousness as something quite other than a transfigurative hero—he entered the culture as a source of gothic dread himself, a living metaphor of the sins white Americans had so fiercely resisted. The dread of and puzzlement over blackness had long been part of the Euro-American tradition since the time of Shakespeare when Elizabethan explorers were discovering Africa and African tribes whose customs, rituals, social structures and skin color they could not understand. Through a blend of cultural chauvinism, eighteenth century conceits of natural science, and metaphorical traditions, white Euro-Americans developed a matrix of damning racial thought: Social domination generated racial myth, and racial myth justified and encouraged social domination.[19]

Blackness entered the literature of Hawthorne and Poe, as well as a multitude of other white American writers, as a common metaphor for sin, corruption, dirtiness, and moral depravity. Although both

Hawthorne and Poe revealed little social consciousness,[20] they knew quite well that the black man lived within the American consciousness as a nightmare. Poe's Dirk Peters, the black character created for *The Narrative of A. Gordon Pym,* and who Fiedler calls "a nightmare our of our racial beginnings,"[21] was a dark figure literally and mythically, who tempted Pym from the restraint of civilized behavior. Hawthorne created for his story "The Birthmark" the swarthy Aminadab, descendant of Caliban, who lusted after the virginal body of a white woman. In The Scarlet Letter the characters speak of the "Black Man who haunts the forest," and who marks Hester Prynne with the symbol of her sexual sin, or so she says.

Hawthorne perceived that good and evil were not necessarily discrete units—good over here, evil over there—as was typical of a more sentimental gothicism, and that perhaps significantly influenced Wright. Both could co-exist and confound each other. Hawthorne showed Wright the way into the complexity of the soul. This was a crucial event in terms of the way Wright could deal with racial conflict, since the separate social existences of blacks and whites, the sharply contrasting physical color, and the contrasting social positions tended to validate in the white mind the objective separation of good and evil—good/white over here, evil/black over there. The whites in *Native Son* certainly perceive what has happened as being true to the Manichean conflict between good and evil, light and dark, head and heart, and restraint and lust. The white masses in *Native Son* are enraged, for they have been "victimized" by the demon from the inner city wilderness; that is the white perspective of the gothic.

In *Native Son* Wright could disassemble such naive notions and perceive blackness as something inside the white head. The black menace was a self-willed and self-created menace that the dominant race used to sustain its domination, rather than an outside menace—a dark force from the wilderness—of whose evil the whites were unwilled recipients. However, what Wright could do that Hawthorne could not was know the gothic dread of whites *from the inside.* As an American black man Wright was the dread. He was in a position, then, to re-write the American gothic mode to suit an Afro-American context. Through the character of Bigger Thomas Wright tried to force blacks back into the white mind and create a story in which we can see the pathology of race and racial hierarchies as a self-willed creation of an American white psyche desperately wanting to hold on to its power.

Throughout the novel Bigger struggles against the ways the white world defines him. But that world cares little for anything other than the survival of its own myths. Early in the novel Bigger watches the movie *Trader Horn* in which he sees a centuries-old European perception of African culture—savages performing primitive antics—revivified and sanctified by Hollywood for the twentieth century white American public. The blighted neighborhood where Bigger lives may be in the massive urban setting of Chicago, yet nonetheless it is a new wilderness to whites—a place for which whites can summon mythic American values and go on a mission of conquest: to bring out Bigger, the demon in that wilderness, after he has killed Mary. Later a newspaper reports about Bigger, after he is captured, that he is "a beast entirely untouched by the softening influences of modern civilization."[22] There are, in fact, no white characters in *Native Son* who have not enclosed Bigger within a mythos that is fundamentally rooted in the gothic dread of blackness. Even the sanitized visions of Jan Erlone, Boris Max, and Mary Dalton owe much to the notions of noble savagery, a mode of thought which "cleansed" blacks and made them available for appreciation—if viewed from the proper emotional, psychological, or physical distance.

But the single most important moment of mythic enclosure in *Native Son* comes with the killing of Mary Dalton. Dan McCall calls that killing "an act of creation. . . . It is a way of escaping all the negatives in [Bigger's] life."[23] Bigger himself believed that "he had murdered and created a new life for himself" after he had killed Mary.[24] But it is at this point, unlike any other in the book, that the power and the will of the white mythos comes to the fore with all of its deadly and insidious force. In that scene Bigger accidentally smothers a drunken and sexually aroused Mary when he is frightened by the appearance of Mrs. Dalton in Mary's room. Since she is blind Mrs. Dalton cannot see them, but Bigger covers Mary's face with a pillow to keep her quiet. It has been critically axiomatic to read that scene as an objectification of the taboo Bigger, and blacks in general, felt about the power of the white world. As the lawyer Max suggests in defending Bigger, Mary's death was unwittingly caused by the depraved sense of social order of the white race. "We planned the murder of Mary Dalton," Max insists in his defense of Bigger.[25]

But as the gothic forms of that scene develop, one must wonder how unwitting the death of Mary really was. Was her death a way to draw the white mythos into the light of the sun, where it could be confronted and slain? If so, then her death indeed was an act of creation in which Bigger created a self apart from the dictates of white mythology. But I would suggest that her death was more a means for the white mythos to assert and renew its power. Mary's death, like Antaeus being dashed to the ground, could rouse the mythos to an even greater strength than before.

In its fundamental structure the scene is a straightforward telling of a gothic seduction: a virginal young white girl, appropriately named Mary, is on the verge of being sexually taken by the "beast," the bogeyman who haunts the dreams of young girls to both terrify and arouse them. Before she is "taken," however, a guardian angel appears on the scene—a mother, no less, the icon of goodness and sustainer of domestic and sexual order—apparently to save Mary from that shame. Indeed, Mary is saved, but in the process she is killed (a desirable end, given the alternative of falling prey to the sexual advances of the beast). As we might expect, after her death Mary is consistently portrayed as innocent and unknowing—someone too naive to know better than to be alone with a black man. This, of course, is precisely the sentiment that guides the responses of the whites in *Native Son*—whites as victims of the external presence of objectified evil. It is also a sentiment common to the American gothic form.

We might be tempted, as Boris Max was, to absolve Bigger of full responsibility and place the blame in a knee-jerk sort of way upon the mindless social system that created the fear that led to a killing. But while that may absolve Bigger, it also absolves whites, for such a system is beyond anyone's control. If that were Wright's purpose then he would have written a novel full of pity but woefully lacking in the fear he desired.

Mary's death, however, was no accident. That is the way it had to be. Mary, in fact, is the good girl gone bad. She drinks and smokes, plays around with a Communist, and has a history of upsetting the propriety of the Dalton family (though after her death her image is re-fashioned in a way to appeal to the gothic expectations of the white American public). What mood of gothic sentimentalism may have been developing in that scene is quickly shattered when a gently inquisitive Mrs. Dalton comes near to Mary lying on her bed and cries out in disgust, "You're dead drunk! You *stink* with whiskey!"[26]

But Mary's worst sin, by far, is that *she* is the seducer and is attempting, however drunken her state happens to be, to cross over the line separating light from dark into damnation. In order for Mary to be saved, she had to die, as all seductresses in the trope of the seduction tale must be castigated. But this was more than "mere" seduction—this was something foul to the white mythos. Only Bigger knows what actually happened in Mary's bedroom, and as a young, troublesome black man he had no chance of being believed. Without Mary's death, we have something sleazy; with Mary's death, we have the confirmation of an archetypal dread. Through Mary's death whites can dredge from the depths of their gothic fears all of their racist fury.

Wright casts a shadow of supernatural doubt over the scene when he remarks that Bigger felt "that he had been in the grip of a weird spell" while Mrs. Dalton was in the room and he was smothering Mary.[27] When Bigger is free from the spell, he finds himself confronting a situation where he had acted precisely as the white mythos would have predicted. Bigger, of course, knows the truth: the death was accidental, and there was no rape. But that hardly matters. Mary's death has strengthened the conviction of the white mythos about the black beast because the black beast has raped and killed a young white girl, at least so far as anyone knows, or as far as most whites will interpret. All whites know, presumably, how scenes between black men and white women *had* to be played out. The death of Mary Dalton, then, is not the product of Bigger's fear, but the product of white desire—a sacrifice to sustain its own mythic mystery and power. The scene reveals as much about the dread of whites as it does about the fears of Bigger Thomas.

Before and after his crime Bigger is haunted by Poe-esque images of the sort created out of the madness of Poe's guilty characters, who are haunted into confessions by consciences they had not acknowledged or attended. The white cat, for example, that pounces on Bigger's shoulder in Wright's homage to "The Black Cat" behaves like a familiar who knows what secrets Bigger holds. Each time Bigger thinks to clean out Mary's bones from the furnace where he burned her body, he is stopped by his visions of her blood or of her unburned body lying in the furnace. He is pursued by the eyes of womenhood throughout the novel as they see the crime in his soul. When he helps the drunken Mary up the steps to her bedroom, he notices her "dark eyes [that] looked at him feverishly from deep sockets."[28] After her death, those eyes reappear in the cat (a female), who had eyes like "two green burning pools,"[29] and even in his murdered girlfriend Bessie:

> then a dreadful thought rendered him incapable of action. Suppose Bessie was not as she had sounded when the brick hit her? Suppose, when he turned on the flashlight, he would see her lying there staring at him with those round large black eyes, her bloody mouth open in awe and wonder and pain and accusation.[30]

These images suggest that even before Bigger killed Mary the will to such an action existed unarticulated in his subconscious. If so, then one might suggest that Bigger perhaps had acted out of free will. By accepting responsibility he disempowers the mythos of the white race. Bigger perhaps even manages to articulate that notion with his famous closing statement "But what I killed for, I am!"[31] Max is horrified, and justifiably so, since Bigger's responsibility diminishes his theories (and perhaps pricks at his own gothic dread).

Yet such responsibility had always eluded Bigger before. Moreover nowhere in the scene of the actual killing does Wright offer any suggestions that Mary's death occurred out of any response other than passivity—fear of acting, rather than impulse to act. If so, then we cannot say Bigger's crime was an act of creation. We must also keep in mind McCall's assessment that the white man's fantasies were inside the head of Wright. That is also true of Bigger. The Poe-esque images are not emerging from his conscience, but are being imposed from without—they are creations of the white mythos. Like Mary's death, the images that haunt Bigger come from pursuit of the white mythos. Those images ultimately compel him to do what the white mythos wanted—accept responsibility for a crime he did not commit and accept it in such a way as to confirm the values of the white mythos.

The images do not elicit a maddened confession out of him, and in fact have little to do with guilt at all. They compel Bigger to play out his role to its inevitable conclusion. If Bigger could have just left Mary on a couch—if he could have stayed calm in the bedroom or fled—if he could have rid the furnace of the ashes and Mary's bones . . . . Bigger constantly deceives himself into believing that he has got away with something, that he has created his own hidden niche in the world. He can never quite believe that his actions would have a larger meaning to the massive white world, and that is his fatal calculation.

As Bigger insists, the whites "would never think that he had done it; not a meek black boy like him."[32] This is Bigger's self-defense, and his self-deceit.

When the body is discovered, the white world is galvanized into unified action; in response to Bigger's crime whites vent their anger upon blacks en masse.[33] More revealing are the newspaper accounts written about Bigger, not for the attitude which they reveal, but for their lack of surprise at Bigger's actions. The sort of crime that Bigger has supposedly committed "is easy to imagine," the story states. Bigger is categorized as one of those "depraved types of Negroes," implying that whites had a well-ordered classification system ready to explain the likes of Bigger. The paper is even ready to offer a "sensible" explanation: he has " . . . a minor portion of white blood in his veins, a mixture which generally makes for a criminal and intractable nature"; throughout the article blacks in general are talked about as a race of potential rapists.[34] Bigger's notion that none would take notice is completely false. What Bigger did provided American whites with the means to sate their expectations.

In *Native Son* Wright was not interested in hinting at or posing a solution to a problem. He was more interested in revealing the terrifying power that held both whites and blacks in its grip. And it was indeed a most terrifying power—cruel enough to sacrifice one of its own to serve its own ends. It demanded and commanded ritualistic behavior.

At the end of *Native Son* the old order of white supremacy has not been overturned; it has been given fulfillment. With that in mind Bigger's final declaration, "what I killed for, I *am*!," is more a final cry of gothic terror than of triumph, since what he killed for was the confirmation of that white mythos. With his final words Bigger tells us exactly of the horror that lived in the heart of the white mythos. In an odd way the gothic achieves the rationality Wright so desired, because the gothic form revealed the emotional and mystical entrapment that possessed both blacks and whites. In the end Wright was able to use the gothic to declare that such damaging mystical notions had no place in a rational, secular, civilized world. Those notions only belonged in the backwaters of primitive racial enmity, of the kind that would goad Bigger and the white race to violence.

Notes

1. Houston A. Baker, Jr., *Singers of Daybreak: Studies in Black American Literature* (Washington, D.C.: Howard University Press, 1983), 3.
2. Leslie A. Fiedler, *Waiting for the End* (New York: Stein and Day, 1964), 107.
3. Richard Wright, *Native Son* (New York: Harper and Row, 1940), xxxiv. All subsequent citations from *Native Son* are from this edition.
4. Dan McCall, "The Bad Nigger," excerpted from *The Example of Richard Wright* (New York, 1969, in *Twentieth Century Interpretations of Native Son*, ed. Houston A. Baker, Jr. Englewood Cliffs, N.J.: Prentice-Hall, Inc.1972), 84.
5. Cited in Houston A. Baker, Jr., "Sightings: Black Historical Consciousness and the New Harbors of the Fifties," *The Journey Back: Issues in Black Literature and Criticism* (Chicago: University of Chicago Press, 1980), 63.
6. *Native Son*, 354.
7. For a comparative discussion of the European and American forms of the gothic, see "Part One: Prototypes and Early Adaptations," Leslie A. Fiedler, *Love and Death in the American Novel* (New York: Dell Publishing, 1966).
8. Frederick Douglass, *My Bondage and My Freedom* (New York: Miller, Orton & Mulligan, 1855), 107–108.
9. Ibid., 80.
10. *Native Son*, 16.
11. Ibid., 33.
12. Ibid., 45.
13. Ibid., 47.
14. Ibid., 48.
15. Ibid., 63.
16. Ibid., 364.
17. Ibid., 35.
18. James Baldwin, "Many Thousands Gone," excerpted from *Notes of a Native Son* (Boston, 1955, in *Twentieth Century Interpretations of Native Son*), 51.
19. For a more complete discussion of the origins of American racial attitudes towards blacks, see Winthrop D. Jordan, *White Over*

Black: American Attitudes Toward the Negro 1550–1812 (Chapel Hill: University of North Carolina Press, 1968).

20. In his *American Notebooks*, for example, Hawthorne commented "I find myself rather more of an abolitionist in feeling than in principle," suggesting the same sort of waffling about slavery of which many white Americans were guilty—manumission was right and proper, so long as it did not threaten the socio-economic status quo. See *The American Notebooks* (Columbus: Ohio State University Press, 1972), 112.

21. Fiedler, *Love and Death*, 397.

22. *Native Son*, 260.

23. McCall, 87.

24. *Native Son*, 101.

25. Ibid., 363.

26. Ibid., 85.

27. Ibid., 86.

28. Ibid., 81.

29. Ibid., 90.

30. Ibid., 223.

31. Ibid., 392.

32. Ibid., 179.

33. Ibid., 228–229.

34. Ibid., 260, 261, 261.

Richard Wright's "Big Boy Leaves Home" and a Tale from Ovid: A Metamorphosis Transformed

Michael Atkinson

There is an ache in reading Richard Wright's fiction, and we feel it from first to last. It is the ache of difference, of distance between what might and should be possible for the human, and what fate and circumstance impose when that human is an outsider, is black. It is paradigmatically present in one of Wright's earliest stories, one of his most enduring and frequently anthologized, "Big Boy Leaves Home." This story continues to move us and be the object of our study, not only because of its starkly accurate social detail, a closely woven fabric of dialect and milieu, and its skill in capturing the black experience of the American South in the first third of this century, but because it has as well a particular, and until now silent, relationship with myth, no less effective for being mute. The story is grounded in a link to myth far more specific than the broad notion of The American Myth (in which it certainly participates) or even the timeless, generalized archetypal motifs that punctuate and shape all literature (although there is no shortage of thresholds and wombs, serpents and guardians here). The pleasures and terrors of "Big Boy Leaves Home" are modeled on a classical myth, one of the most affecting and familiar—the myth of Actaeon and Diana. Rereading Wright's story in this connection can add a depth and resonance to our experience, framing the sense of social realism in a larger ontology. The parallels—and the divergences— between the myth and the story play off one another, creating a denser texture of emotional response and a suppler philosophical grasp as we read and reflect.

The similarities, and some of the differences, between the two can be foregrounded by setting the outlines of the myth and the story side by side. In Ovid's *Metamorphoses*, the most complete and accessible telling, the tale of Actaeon runs thus.[1] Actaeon and his companions are out hunting at mid-day when Actaeon calls an end to the chase since "Our nets and spears / Drip with the blood of our successful hunting" (Ovid 61). Nearby, in a grotto pool nestled in a valley, the goddess Diana, herself tired from hunting, disrobed and disarmed, bathes with her maidens. Two nymphs are pouring urns full of water over her, when quite by accident, Actaeon, now separated from his companions, comes upon the idyllic scene. Finding no weapon at hand, Diana flings a handful of the pond's water on the hapless hunter, taunting, "Tell people you have seen me, / Diana, naked! Tell them if you can!" (Ovid 62). As he flees from the scene, he is by stages transformed into a stag, a metamorphosis he does not comprehend, though he marvels at his own speed, until he pauses at a pool for refreshment. There he "finally sees, reflected, / his features in a quiet pool. 'Alas!' / He tries to say, but has no words." Stunned, he hears his hounds approach. "The whole pack, with the lust of blood upon them / Come baying. . . Actaeon, once pursuer / Over this very ground, is now pursued. . . He would cry / 'I am Actaeon . . .' / But the words fail" (Ovid 63). The hounds set upon him "And all together nip and slash and fasten / Till there is no more room for wounds." Meanwhile, his companions arrive at the spectacle, call for him, and rue that he is missing the good show. "And so he died, and so Diana's anger / Was satisfied at last" (Ovid 64).

When we look at the story of Big Boy, the similarities are striking—and once they are established, the divergences are revealing as well. As the story begins, Big Boy and his three companions, playing hooky from school, wander through the woods, laughing and singing a risqué song about seeing one's mother without her underwear. One suggests that they go to the swimming hole on old man Harvey's property. Initially reluctant, Big Boy finally consents after a tussle with the other three and they cross the fence, shed their clothes and enjoy a swim in the cool water that hot afternoon. As they rest naked on the bank, enjoying the sunshine, they hear a cry—"Oh!" —and see a white woman coming over the rise, looking in shock at the black boys. Startled and afraid, the boys start to flee, but Big Boy wants to go back for their clothes, piled under a tree near which the white woman now stands. As he and his companion Bobo approach the tree, she shrieks, summoning the man she is with, who arrives on the scene with a rifle. He shoots two of the boys and is about to shoot the third when Big Boy wrests the gun from him and hits him with it. Though warned, the man lays hold of the rifle and tries to take it back. Big Boy shoots him. He and Bobo, his one remaining companion, flee the scene, don clothes, and return to their respective homes. Big Boy's family, extracting from him only confused and fragmentary details of what has happened, summon some of the elders of the black community, but they are powerless to protect or hide him. One suggests that he hide until morning, then catch a ride north in his son's truck, bound for Chicago. Big Boy says he will hide in a hole on a hillside full of kilns the boys themselves dug earlier that summer. He asks them to tell Bobo to join him and runs for the kilns. There, he fantasizes the struggle to come. When the white men do arrive, they have brought their hounds and their women with them. The hounds find Bobo and the men mutilate him to the singing cheers of the women. They tar and feather him, and then set him afire with gasoline as Big Boy, remembering that "you could not see into the dark if you were standing in the light," witnesses the whole scene (Wright 48). Satisfied, the mob leaves, and Big Boy sleeps the dank night in the kiln, wakes the next morning and hears the sound of Will's truck. Unable to find his voice at first, he finally utters Will's name, enters the truck and hides in the back, bound for the north, for Chicago, leaving forever his home and his people.

The points of congruence here are striking: the easy companionship, the idyllic setting, the pond, nakedness, discovery, the power of the woman, the wrenching transformation of a life, the hero's muteness, the hounds, mutilation. And the divergences, too, are striking, even after we have taken into account the necessary dilution of power and difference that must take place when a myth that includes the gods is shifted to a strictly human theatre. Most notably, in the story it is the woman who sees the men naked, rather than the reverse. The presence, and murder, of the male protector is an element the story adds—and then curiously effaces. And of course there is the pluralization of protagonism and the sharing of agony in the later story. But in both congruence and divergence, the myth Ovid tells provides for Wright's story a strong commentary in counterpoint. It subtlizes, extends, and validates what we feel as we read, deepens and clarifies what we understand. If we compare the crucial structural stages of the parallel stories, we can best see what the one has made of the other.

Both heroes begin in a kind of innocence. If the joy of a general kill rings a little violent to the modern sensibility, we need only remember the unqualified delight in large kill that so pleases the huntress Diana herself, not to mention similar occasions in the Gawain poet and in Faulkner. And too, Actaeon has called a halt to the sport, unwilling to let the zest of the hunt become bloodlust in excess of need and moderate pleasure. He and his companions are, in the context of their story, innocent, at rest and carefree. Likewise, Wright's story opens with an idyll still within the borders of adolescent innocence, though perhaps in some ways nearer the line. They are playing hooky, hardly a crime, and on a warm day they walk in the woods and giggle at the scatological jokes that seem the timeless staple of adolescence. Mixed with this is the singing of the familiar hymn about the train that is bound for glory. But the story actually opens with a playful hint of sexual impropriety; the boys sing a dirty song:

> *Yo mama don wear no drawers,*
> *Ah seena when she pulled em off,*
> *N she washed em in alcohol,*
> *N she hung em in the hall.*

Stuck for the next line, they ponder rhymes. It is Big Boy that comes up with the solution:

> *N then she put em back on her QUALL!* (Wright 238)

This ribald innocence, however, is given edge when we recall the myth, for clearly it is as taboo in the realistic world to see the naked mother as it is to see the naked goddess in the world of myth. This is the forbidden woman, the forbidden vision, and it is Big Boy who names the forbidden part: "quall," a folk word with clear links to the "queynte" and "quoniam" of Middle English. They have—he has—crossed a boundary, later literally marked by their crossing the fence onto the forbidden property of old man Harvey.[2] So there is, it seems, a little less innocence in the trespass of the young black men than in Actaeon's. He, at least, is unwitting, though the landscape into which he wanders is profoundly feminine: a pool in a grotto in a valley with an archway above the bathing goddess and her urn-bearing nymphs.

Another key element in the idyllic time before the shattering dislocation is the communal friendship in both tales. Both Actaeon and Big Boy begin in the midst of their companions. The kind of easy union that both experience is of the essence of the idyllic moment, the core of which is the operative principle of non-differentiation, a lack of otherness. Actaeon simply wanders away, taking his own path home after the hunt. His separation from his companions is as swift and initially nonchalant as Big Boy's is protracted and agonizing. But both lead to tragic isolation. The isolation of Big Boy proceeds by degrees. The other three jump him after he is reluctant to cross the fence to the swimming hole. Big Boy wins the fight by grasping Bobo's neck in a chokehold, forcing him to call off the others. Though this might for a moment seem like an antagonism between the two, it is rather like part of a brother battle after which these two are more closely united, and differentiated from the others, a fact presaged by the common alliteration of their names. At the pond, Bobo tries to throw Big Boy in. They lock in a struggle that is also a bonding, and Lester and Buck push the two of them in together.

The vestige of communality among the four is for the last time invoked after they have finished their exuberant swimming and splashing and are sunning on a bank by the side of the pool. Though in the forbidden territory, and conscious of the other and the differentiation he brings (they wonder, "Whut would yuh do ef ol man Harveyd come erlong right now?" "Run like hell!"), the talk is easy, and suggestive of a larger and more profound, political communality.

> Far away a train whistled.
> "There goes number seven!"
> "Heading fer up Noth!"
> "Blazin it down the line!"
> "Lawd, Ahm goin Noth some day."
> "Me too, man."
> "They say colored folks up Noth is got ekual rights."
> (Wright 26–27)

This political promise—the faintly present vision of equality and justice against which the terrifying degradation to come can alone be measured—is underscored by the most lyric passage in the story, which follows immediately. It is utterly unlike anything else in the piece.

> They grew pensive. A black winged butterfly hovered at the
> water's edge. A bee droned. From somewhere came the sweet
> scent of honeysuckles. Dimly they could hear the sparrows
> twittering in the woods. They rolled from side to side, letting
> sunshine dry their skins and warm their blood. They plucked
> blades of grass and chewed them. (Wright 27)

This experience of oneness among themselves, of unreflective unity
with nature, culminates the idyll. It is riven and terminated by the
intrusion of the ultimate otherness in the very next line. "Oh!" It
could be an exclamation of pure surprise. But it is not. It could be a
cry of delight at the beauty of these four young men. But it is not.
For this single word is uttered by the one who is the ultimate principle
of difference and differentiation in the story. Not black, not male.

> A white woman, poised on the edge of the opposite
> embankment, stood directly in front of them, her hat in her
> hand and her hair lit by the sun. (Wright 27)

In a muted but familiar motif symbolizing a threatened loss of virginal
purity, her hat is off, her hair revealed. And like Diana the virgin moon
goddess, this woman (whose name, Bertha, means "bright") is a creature
of reflected light, her hair lit by the sun. As in Actaeon's case, this
clear and radiant glimpse could be the culmination of the idyll rather
than the shattering of it, were it not for the absolute difference between
the seer and the seen. The difference between gods and humans is so
great a gulf that unmediated vision of pure and naked divinity threatens
life itself, from Ovid and Exodus to *Space Odyssey 2001*. The
ontological difference in the myth is reflected in the sociological
difference in the story: the same principle operates, a radical difference
on the scale of being.

Is it axiomatic to say that before the mother the conscious child is
always guilty? Big Boy and Actaeon share a guilt that is not born of
intent but of condition, and the condition of each is marked by his
name. "Actaeon" means "shore dweller," one who must not violate the
waters even with vision, and "Big Boy" marks clearly that he is a
perpetual manchild in a land without promise. In *Violence and the
Sacred* René Girard proposes that it is not inequality that causes primary
violence, as today we would like to believe, but the very breakdown of
inequality that leads to strife and bloodshed (49–52). And certainly that

is true in both the myth and the story. Actaeon sees the goddess naked, as he might be privileged to see an ordinary woman. And Bertha sees the naked boys as she might see her own younger relatives—cause for embarrassment perhaps, but not for terror or revenge. However, in each case, the seeing is not ordinary; it casts itself across the barrier of difference and momentarily threatens to obscure it in the act of mutual seeing. Violence must ensue.

It is important to remember that in both cases, though the act is hedged around with sexuality, the crime is one of vision rather than sex, though clearly the two are often related in practice. And of course the differing directions of the vision, and the nakedness before it, constitute one of the chief distinctions between the story and the myth. This casts into bold relief the fact that in the society of this fiction, the black man must not have the power to *see*; for to see, to hold another in one's gaze as existential phenomenology describes it, is to give him meaning, to objectify him (Sartre 228 ff., 339, 375–379). To fix another in one's gaze is, at root, a powerful gesture, for in doing so, one defines and dehumanizes one's object, demotes him in the scale of being, makes him a thing. But since the other is not in fact merely an object and can by free action escape denomination, final objectification must be culminated in literally making an object of the one caught in the gaze, sadism and killing being the obvious alternatives, as both myth and story demonstrate. Again, what is an ontological difference in levels of being in the myth is recast as a sociological difference in the story. But while Actaeon's crime is seeing, objectifying, what he should not see, Big Boy's crime, and the crime of his companions, is not seeing, but being seen; ironically *their crime is synonymous with their power-lessness*, their impotence as humans.

Seen, the young men's "hands instinctively cover[ed] their groins" (Wright 27). Big Boy attempts the obvious human act—to recover his clothes, to be seen only as he would wish to be seen, to cover himself, as the woman he confronts is clothed. He is in effect resisting metamorphosis into an "animal." Clothing and disrobing have long been used as symbols of transformation, from the hooding of Ph.D.'s and the complex formulas for assembling a bride's gear, to the investing (and defrocking) of priests.[3] In his rush for the clothes Big Boy is joined by Bobo, while Lester and Buck hang back. But appropriately, if ironically, their clothing lies at the foot of the tree next to which the woman now stands, as if symbolic of her power to see them only as naked and threatening, to enforce their metamorphosis into animals. Big Boy assures her that they only "wanna git [their] clothes" (Wright 28). But as Bobo retrieves the bundle, her transforming gaze, her fear, is now extended in the lethal power of the man she summons (in myth, one would say her votary and protector). Jim, her fiancé, thoroughly dressed in an Army uniform and shouldering a rifle, shoots Buck, who falls into the pool (the mythic locus of the goddess's power), and Lester, who falls with his forehead on the toe of the woman's shoe in a perverse mockery of worship. Big Boy and Bobo refuse this obeisance. As Jim tries to shoot Bobo, Big Boy wrests the gun from him. Undaunted, the white man attempts to regain the weapon, is shot in the process, and the two young men flee, isolated forever from their dead comrades, united in their fear and their crime.

Recollecting the terms of the original myth will enhance our understanding of the shape of Big Boy's flight. Although the course of Actaeon's story runs swiftly, it is important to remember that there are two woundings: the transformative sprinkling with pondwater, which removes his humanity, and the obliterative tearing by the dogs' teeth, which destroys the last form and vestige of life. Actaeon's first wound is itself twofold. He flees the goddess with a speed that amazes him, only realizing that he has been transformed into a stag when he pauses

> and finally sees, reflected,
> His features in a quiet pool. "Alas!"
> He tries to say, but has no words. He groans,
> The only speech he has, and the tears run down
> Cheeks that are not his own. (Ovid 63)

It is significant that Diana taunts him not with his change of shape but specifically with the loss of speech she knows he will suffer: "Tell them you have seen me, / Diana, naked! Tell them if you can!" (Ovid 61). This second aspect of Actaeon's first wounding, his muteness, serves a dual function. It ensures that the vision of the naked goddess will never reach the consciousness of the human community and it removes the last possible outer sign of his humanity; only his thoughts are now human.

Though more stadial and protracted, the wounding of Big Boy also occurs in two major movements. In the first wounding, he too has been sprinkled, with the blood of his fallen comrades—and their deaths constitute for him a vicarious wounding. Big Boy's demotion to animal has perhaps been more fully sensed at the swimming hole than Actaeon's at the pond, but his muteness is revealed only gradually. In Wright's story, there is no imagistic counterpart of the reflecting pool, as there are for so many other elements of the myth. But there is a structural counterpart: his visit home. He too pauses in his flight from the goddess, pauses at the shack of his parents. As his mother questions him, we sense the echo of Actaeon's look in the pool:

> "Whut's the matter, Big Boy?"
> Mutely, he looked at her. Then he burst into tears. She came and felt the scratches on his face. (Wright 32)

Inarticulate and confused, he cannot give a coherent account of what has happened, and his mother must extract the fragments of the experience from him in a chaotic order. She is unable to understand the seriousness of what has happened until Big Boy, having already mentioned the three deaths, mumbles, "We wuz swimmin, Ma. N the white woman . . . " "*White* woman?" she cries, and suddenly the impact of the crime is full upon her. Explaining to his father, she arrests his attention and brings the matter into focus in the same way: "Saul, its a *white* woman!" And he in turn conveys the same emphasis to the hastily called council of elders (Wright 32, 34, 38). That the white woman's mere presence on the scene so immediately dwarfs the significance of the killing is a striking indicator of the power of the goddess. Big Boy's muteness has social significance, for there is no moral grammar in which his case could be made, his sentence lifted. In the white woman's extended gaze, there is no hope of innocence. Like the pool at which Actaeon pauses, the family can only reflect his desperate situation. They cannot harbor him, for to do so would be to bring destruction on themselves in their powerlessness. But one of the elders does suggest that his own son, a truck driver, could smuggle Big Boy north, if only he could be hidden until morning. In his last utterances there, Big Boy proposes to pass the night hiding in one of the kilns he dug in the hillside out past the town; and he asks that Bobo be told of his plan, that he may join him in flight.

As the next section of Big Boy's story opens, a dramatic shift in narrative is immediately apparent. The previous parts of the story have been dominated by dialogue, using narrative perspective mainly to splice the conversations together. Though there are very good reasons to shift to an emphasis on the narrative voice (quiet is necessary if Big Boy is to remain hidden; there is no one for him to talk to), this silencing of the protagonist, and of all black voices in general, also carries the symbolic weight of the wound of muteness. And as is the case with Actaeon, in this silence, we hear for the very first time the thoughts of the protagonist.[4] In Actaeon's instance, these thoughts ricochet between fear, shame, and pleading. Big Boy's blossom as alternating fantasies of an idyllic past, of ignoble defeat, and (primarily) of heroic defiance: he remembers the fun of play while digging these kilns with his three companions, imagines being torn apart by the vicious pack of bloodhounds he is almost certain are on his trail, and envisions standing off his white pursuers, a defiance to be memorialized in newspaper headlines: "NIGGER KILLS DOZEN OF MOB BEFO LYNCHED! . . . TRAPPED NIGGER SLAYS TWENTY BEFO KILLED!" (Wright 258). These may be the adolescent and exaggerated fantasies of one at bay, but they are also a poignant reminder of the interiority of the hero, the memories and aspirations that make up his soul, the very inner freedom which the objectifying gaze seeks to eradicate. This desperate play of this silent interiority is interrupted by the voices of the pursuing whites.

Hiding in the kiln, the womb-like cavity in the earth which he has killed an inhabiting snake to gain, the silent Big Boy listens to the rising crescendo of voices. Unwittingly they bring him news: some of the lynch mob have put the torch to his parents' shack, the last communal reflector in which his humanity could be measured socially. And too the voices bear the sanction of their mission: "Ef they git erway notta woman in this town would be safe" (Wright 46). No matter what the physical case, the symbolic virginity of the white woman can be perpetuated, like Diana's, if she is not threatened with the touch of the black man. Bertha herself and the other women of the town are there to witness the sacrificial purification. The mission is clear: no mention of the murder of Jim Harvey is made, effectively eliminating him again from the symbolic economy of the story, retaining the myth's focus on the crime against the feminine.

The hounds approach. They have found the snake that Big Boy killed, and it seems that his discovery is imminent. The reigning irony of the Actaeon myth—the hero terribly torn apart by his own hounds—is missing here, in two ways. First, though of course a black man might well own hounds, in the myth they figure as symbols of the hero's power, and here the black man is powerless. Wright even has Big Boy think of the whites and the bloodhounds synonymously— terrifying, atavistic and without human values—"Gawddam them white folks! Thas all they wuz good fer, t run a nigger down lika rabbit!" (Wright 44). Further dissipating the irony, it is not Big Boy that is discovered, but Bobo, who also had silently taken up hiding on the hillside. Though Big Boy has imagined his own being torn by the hounds, it will not be his to endure directly.

As the mob presses forward to see the prize the dogs have found, the women raise their voices in song. Big Boy, inwardly compelled to witness though aching at the sight, shrinks from the light cast by the fire the mob has built. But then he remembers an important fact which might well serve as the epigraph for the whole story: "*you could not see into the dark, if you were standing in the light*" (Wright 48; italics mine). In the white mob's consciousness, nothing "inside" the black man could be seen. His interiority, his soul, is invisible. In the light of their fire, Bobo appears, even to Big Boy, as just a "long dark spot" (Wright 48). To Big Boy, and perhaps Wright, the souls of the whites are similarly obscured—but he does not have the capacity to *see* them in that primal, defining, life-altering sense.

The mob crowds around to the call, "LES GIT SOURVINEERS!" (Wright 49). They will remember him by dismembering him, taking a finger, an ear—what else?—to recall the night on which they very non-metaphorically, quite literally, turned a human being into an object. This ritual tearing asunder—which the Greeks called *sparagmos*—is one of the most consistent features of tragic and ironic myth: Actaeon, Pentheus and Orpheus rent, Osiris scattered, Christ's body pierced and sacramentally distributed, Oedipus and Gloucester blind, Shylock calling for his pound of flesh. But, as Northrop Frye points out, *sparagmos* signifies not only the disfiguration or dismemberment of a hero, but also the fragmentation or disappearance of the heroic—"the sense that heroism or effective action are absent" or for the time impossible (192). That double sense counts in Wright's story: Bobo is mutilated and Big Boy is completely powerless to act heroically to save him. The thought never crosses his mind, even in the sort of fantasy he was able to sustain earlier. The scene is the story's most humiliating: it is a scene of ritual or metaphorical as well as literal killing, for something in Big Boy dies too.

Actaeon also suffered such a wounding, at the teeth of the dogs that were once his.

> So they run him
> To stand at bay until the whole pack gathers
> And all together nip and slash and fasten
> Till there is no more room for wounds. (Ovid 64)

"Till there is no more room for wounds"—surely this is one of the most heart-rending lines of the tale. And one of the most ontologically significant. For when there is no more room for wounds, there is no form, even at the physical level, no identity to support those wounds. With no ground against which the wounds can be gauged or measured, woundedness itself becomes a condition of blank, of non-entity. The only ground of being which Actaeon had left was history—lodged in the memory of his companions and family. But even this is symbolically destroyed for Big Boy, the shack burnt, his friends dead or dying. Disfigurement does not complete the *sparagmos* of Bobo; he must be transformed, metamorphosed, into a non-being on whom there is "no more room for wounds." And how does one make the black man into a non-entity? By denying his difference, of which there are two methods: by covering him with a caricature of his own blackness and by robbing him of his blackness, making him a parody of the white. Both of these seemingly contradictory maneuvers occur in the subsequent tarring and feathering of Bobo, as it is witnessed by Big Boy.

Since he is seeing things in the light of the mob's fire—that is, as they see them—he is only able to see Bobo as a "long dark spot" when the mob pours tar over him. They have given him—made him over in—their own parodic cast of darkness, blackness: again, "You could not see into the dark if you were standing in the light." And then the feathers. After the tar has horribly accentuated his blackness and his suffering, symbolically enough Bobo is covered with feathers. With this applied whiteness, he is denied his own identity, both racially and humanly: he is made to look like a ridiculous animal, in a now even more powerful recapitulation of the metamorphosis at the pond.

But that is not the final transformation. For once blackness has been travestied, then covered with whiteness, a new and extinguishing blackness must rid the mind of all memories save the physical, "objective," souvenirs. And so Bobo is doused with gasoline and set afire, like the shack of Big Boy's parents. He has become truly a wound that leaves no place for wounds, black again as the mob would have him black—a non-entity, beyond recognition. For Big Boy, both friends and family have been eradicated. Diana taunted Actaeon to "tell *them* if you can," thus placing a premium on preventing a social grounding for Actaeon's vision; so the mob in Wright's story is keen to eliminate anything which might permit a social validation for Big Boy's seeing.

After Big Boy has witnessed and numbly internalized Bobo's death, he himself is threatened with discovery by one of the hounds. This dog he takes by the neck and, despite its vigor, strangles it—a token vengeance on the mob which only amounts to a defense of his increasingly isolated self. Again, the *sparagmos* or dismemberment of Bobo is matched by the enforced *sparagmos* or disappearance of effective action in Big Boy. He can preserve himself, no more.

Big Boy wakes curled beside the dog he has killed. The morning also brings the sound of the truck. This night of *sparagmos* and muteness is broken, if not dispelled, when Big Boy attempts to speak: "He tried to call to Will, but his dry throat would make no sound" (Wright 51). In a second try, he finds his voice, and with it contacts Will, whose name points to Big Boy's only remaining means and motive for survival. He has eluded the fate of Actaeon—at least on a literal level. And the familiar motifs of the rebirth archetype appear to reinforce this: after Big Boy emerges from the womb-like kiln, utters his first cry, and joins his fate to Will, a rooster crows, and rays of sunlight penetrate even into the back of the truck in which he hides.

But there is a negative element here too. In the kiln, he has been hardened. It is will alone that sustains him, not feeling or compassion or justice. Though the ultimate wounding has been vicarious, it is deep. The numbness that pervades his experience radiates out from this story and informs Wright's subsequent fiction. As we know from Wright's autobiographical account of his life previous to writing this story, he had few illusions that a move north could bring unalloyed good. The fact that Wright's later protagonists often grounded their sense of liberation and worth in a gratuitous violence quite equivalent to what the whites perpetrate here soberly mutes any tendency to romanticize the story's ending. The survival in this story is a survival numbed by violence it has internalized, and that numbness only increases in the fiction that follows. To that degree, in the story as in the myth, the goddess has her victory.

Ontology and difference, seeing and being seen, idyll and isolation, speech and silence, transformation and wounding—these are the structures of understanding that emerge to guide us when we bring Richard Wright's story into alignment with its mythic source. In their crosscut, they give us a new and deepened perspective on the human condition as it is portrayed in our century, and twenty centuries before.

References

Frye, Northrop. *Anatomy of Criticism: Four Essays.* Princeton: Princeton University Press, 1957.
Girard, René. *Violence and the Sacred.* Trans. Patrick Gregory. Baltimore: Johns Hopkins University Press, 1977.
Ong, Walter J. "A Dialectic of Aural and Objective Correlatives," *Critical Theory Since Plato.* Ed. Hazard Adams. New York: Harcourt, 1971, 1159–1166.
Ovid, *Metamorphoses,.* Trans. Rolfe Humphries. Bloomington: Indiana University Press, 1964.
Sartre, Jean-Paul. *Being and Nothingness.* Trans. Hazel E. Barnes. Secaucus: Citadel, 1956.
Wright, Richard. *Uncle Tom's Children.* New York: Harper, 1940, 1965.

Notes

1. Although the sheer number of correspondences between Wright and Ovid would argue that he was familiar with the Roman poet's telling, there is no way of knowing which version of Ovid he might have been acquainted with. Because it is now the accepted standard, I have chosen to quote from Rolfe Humphries' translation, even though it was published after Wright wrote the story.
2. Crossing the threshold into the forbidden world is of course one of those omnipresent archetypal motifs which, although it is appropriate to acknowledge them when they figure significantly in the story, do not lie at the core of this more specific analysis of mythological debt. A related association would be the suggestion that the elder Harvey corresponds to the old, now infertile king whose chief function is to proscribe and to hold fast to what he

has. Psychologically, he is the tyrannical father who delimits, owns, and protects the territory in which the "mother" dwells.

3. The awesomeness in seeing the goddess naked can be appreciated by marking its rarity. The most spectacular case in point is the ritual disrobing of Inanna as she descends into the underworld. For her, eventual sacrificial nudity is death.

4. The phenomenology of speech and silence are as suggestive here as the phenomenology of vision. The power of speech is the principal sign by which we intuit the interiority of the other, though that can only be pointed to, never truly revealed to us (Ong 1160). The other, by his speech may demonstrate a subjective freedom—a humanity—which is similar to ours. In life, we can never experience the thoughts of the other, but in fictions of course we can, through indirect and direct quotation of a character's mental processes. In this section of his story, Wright modulates his prose seamlessly between the literate, reportorial voice of the narrator and the colloquial dialect in which Big Boy's thoughts express themselves directly.

Black Girls and Native Sons:
Female Images in Selected Works
by Richard Wright

Nagueyalti Warren

> Black girls, with their giggling and talking, were no longer
> negative creatures who did not 'understand,' but a substratum of
> life whose chief traits were marking time until he and his black
> brothers were old enough to go to them and give them their
> duties.
>
> (Wright, *The Long Dream*)

The subject of female images has often been dismissed as an all too
apparent and pedestrian study. Like the issue of racism, sexism in
literary criticism is viewed as a "limiting moral thesis" (Widmer 13).
Thus, the topic is often mentioned, but only in passing. It is not
enough, however, merely to allude to sexism or explain it as the norm
for a particular historical period. It is necessary to examine the images,
to expose the motivation for them, and to understand their insidious
effects, if lifelike images are ever to emerge.

Blyden Jackson observes that "among the most notable effects of
fiction is its capacity for producing within the limits of the illusion it
creates a world which, even in the sense of the geographer and historian,
can seem, almost literally, very true" ("The Negro's Image of the
Universe as Reflected in His Fiction" 22). If images appear to be real,
then the powerful potential the writer has for shaping attitudes and
beliefs is obvious. "Wright's vision of black men and women . . .
stormed its way into the fabric of American culture with such fury that

its threads form a reference point in the thinking and imagination of those who have yet to read him" (Kent, "Richard Wright: Blackness and the Adventure of Western Culture" 343). The importance and influence of Wright's fiction are probably without question.

The image Richard Wright creates of black female characters in *Native Son* (1940), *Black Boy* (1945), *The Outsider* (1953), *The Long Dream* (1958), and "Long Black Song" is an unwholesome, stereotypical, and degrading collection of what Maria Mootry aptly calls "bitches" and whores." Wright has, perhaps unwittingly, created through the characters of Bessie, Bigger's mother, Cross's mother, his own mother, aunts, grandmother, Gladys in both *The Outsider* and *The Long Dream*, Dot, Emma, etc., a black female who rarely develops beyond the level of a black girl—a counterpart of a black boy. Wright's female characters never do achieve a semblance of womanhood because there is no satisfactory development and portrayal of black manhood in these works. On his artistic landscape, Wright creates castrating mothers; whorish, morally depraved lovers; hysterical, weeping black girls. These characters are only created and sustained as Cross Damon recognizes they can be: "Men made themselves and women were made only through men" (Wright, *The Long Dream* 51).

The sexual stereotypes of black women abound in literature and in other media. Several general categories include the "non-feminine" and what Mae King identifies as "depreciated sex objects" ("The Politics of Sexual Stereotypes" 2). These labels aptly describe the stereotypes found in Wright's work.

The "non-feminine" is a tough, hard-working domestic who assumes the role of matriarch. She is often described as in *The Long Dream* when Tyree says, "That nigger bitch was strong's a horse" (262). The myth of the black matriarchy is a concomitant of the non-feminist image. Matriarchy as it is applied to black American women is an inappropriate term. Black women workers constitute the lowest paid and least powerful group of wage earners. Sociological studies have shown that the black woman rules neither inside nor outside the home environment. Still the myth persists because the nature of myth is socially cued rather than empirically based (King 3). Wright's images help to reinforce the mythology surrounding the black woman.

Bigger's mother, in many respects, is drawn from the non-feminine image. Bigger hates his mother—indeed, his entire family—the narrator tells us, "because he knew that they were suffering and that he was powerless to help them" (*Native Son* 13). Nonetheless, Wright presents other motives for the conflict that exists between Bigger and his mother, i.e., her role as castrator. Instead of the ideal, loving, ego-boosting, and non-aggressive maternal behavior canonized in Western literature, the black mother/matriarch is characterized as insensitive to the male ego, abrasive, and unloving. Bigger's mother continually humiliates him. In one instance she tells him he is "just plain dumb black crazy" (*Native Son* 12); in another she blames their socioeconomic condition on him. "We wouldn't have to live in this garbage dump," she tells him, "if you had any manhood in you" (*Native Son* 12). In Mrs. Thomas, Wright has drawn a black female character who lacks the ability to "grasp subtle principles of conduct, large aspirations, and grand designs" (Keady, "Richard Wright's Women Characters and Inequality" 124). Bigger's mother naively accepts the oppressor's definition of manhood, which equates masculinity with the ability to earn money. Consequently, she tells Bigger, who is reluctant to accept the job as chauffeur for the Daltons, "Bigger, honest, you the most no-countest man I ever seen in all my life" (*Native Son* 12). Mrs. Thomas' dogged insistence on Bigger's accepting the job and providing for the family is ironic in several respects. First, his taking the job—her sending him into the white world—exposes his inability to cope in that environment and results in tragedy. Keady correctly observes that in Wright's novels the "female characters frequently function as vehicles through which the hero's problems and difficulties are further increased" (124). Second, the black mother matriarch finds herself in a precarious predicament. If she shelters the black male, going herself into the white world to work and support the family, she is condemned as castrating, domineering, and too aggressive. If she insists that the black male go, she is insensitive to his masculine pride and ego. It is degrading for the male person to work in a subservient position. But according to popular notions of masculinity and femininity, the truly feminine person is supposed to adapt naturally to roles requiring submissive behavior. Serving through the performance of menial tasks, whether in an oppressive society or in her own home, the female is thought to suffer no loss of ego or self-esteem. Ironically, the nature of the black matriarch is seen as masculine rather than feminine. Consequently, the black woman's working and providing for her family would call for the same denial of ego, pride and aggression required of her male counterpart. Nevertheless, it is acceptable for black females to ingratiate themselves to the Daltons of the world for slave wages and leftovers for their families, because they should not possess the ego, pride, and assertiveness reserved for men in the first place. It is surprising when black women are accused of not knowing the frustration and pain of racism by virtue of the fact that they are women. A startling example appears in *The Long Dream* where Emma's husband tells her, "Emma you a woman and you don't know what life is in the South for black folk" (65). This attitude, sometimes latent, is apparent in the scene about flying in *Native Son*. Bigger is wistful as he watches the airplane with his friends. He resentfully states that "White boys get a chance to do everything" (19). His friend Gus tells him: "If you wasn't black and if you had some money and if they'd let you go to aviation school, you could fly a plane" (20). But Mrs. Thomas' insensitivity is revealed in her observation: "Bigger's setting here like he ain't glad to get a job" (15). While this is an accurate remark (Bigger does not want to be a chauffeur), Wright has created the image of a mother too inept to understand her son's dilemma.

Another aspect of the non-feminine stereotype is sustained by the desexualized, devoutly or fanatically religious image. Bigger's mother with her prophesying and ineffectual praying, Cross Damon's mother with her Christian ethics in *The Outsider*, Granny and Aunt Addie in *Black Boy*, and (to an extent) Emma in *The Long Dream* all represent this part of the non-feminine image. These characters are desexualized by the nature of their physical appearance and sometimes by their age. The description of Fishbelly's teacher typifies the female eunuch—"old, fat, black Mrs. Morrison" (*The Long Dream* 51), as does the mammy image described by Barbara Christian: "black, fat, nurturing, religious, kind but above all strong" (*Black Feminist Criticism* 2). This image is also defined in *The Outsider* when the narrator refers to Cross Damon's "fat, black, religious landlady."

In *Sexual Politics* Kate Millett describes stereotypes that have been the same for black people as they have been for women. She posits:

> Both blacks and women are seen as having inferior intelligence, an instinctual or sensual gratification, an imagined prowess in or affinity for sexuality, a contentment with their own lot which is in accord with a proof of its appropriateness, a wily habit of deceit, and concealment of feeling. Both groups are forced to the same accommodational tactics: an ingratiating or

supplicatory manner invented to please, a tendency to study
those points which the dominant group are subject to influence
or corruption,and an assumed air of helplessness involving
fraudulent appeals for direction through a show of ignorance.
(57)

For the black woman this stereotype operates like a double-edged sword,
wounding her once for being black, and cutting her chances again for
being female.

Both Aunt Addie and Granny display the primitive and childlike
nature that allows them to accept uncritically the oppressor's religion.
Both attempt to force their dogma onto the male figure as a way of
protecting him from a hostile environment. Emma attempts the same
thing with Fishbelly in *The Long Dream*. Their protective behavior is
perceived by males as efforts to castrate them. Cross Damon's mother's
fanaticism is even displayed in the name she selects for him. It is at
once humorous and paradoxical. Mrs. Damon innocently exclaims,
"To think I named you Cross after the cross of Jesus" (*The Outsider*
23). Cross Damon is apparently his mother's cross to bear because he
rejects her moral standards and her religion. This was not, however, due
to her lack of effort:

His [Cross'] first coherent memories had condensed themselves
into an image of a young woman whose hysterically loving
presence had made his imagination conscious of an invisible
God—whose secret grace granted him life. (*The Outsider* 17)

Diane Hoeveler in "Oedipus Agonistes: Mothers and Sons in
Richard Wright's Fiction" states that women do not appear in Wright's
fiction except as mothers or surrogate mother figures (65). A clear
example of Hoeveler's contention is found in *The Long Dream*.
Fishbelly, recovering from a severe illness, clings to his mother

and she, wallowing in guilt, let him. The comfort he drew from
her was sensual in its intensity and it formed the pattern of
what he was to demand later in life from women.When he was a
man and in distress, he would have to have them, but his need
of them would be limited, localized, focused toward obtaining
release, solace. (56)

Darwin Turner also notes that "neither Bigger nor Cross can realize satisfactory companionship with women because both subconsciously regard women essentially as instruments for temporary relief of physical and emotional needs" (317).

Other examples of the mother-son relationship represent the Freudian dimension in Wright's image making. The Oedipal dilemma posited by Freud examines the male child's strong attachment to his mother and the conflicting simultaneous disillusionment because of the mother's sexuality. According to Freud, the male child is forced to accept the female either as an asexual, pure being or as a whore, soiled and deserving of death ("Oedipus Agonistes" 65). Wright's black female characters are either asexual non-feminine or whorish depreciated sex objects.

The literature abounds with existentialist interpretations of Wright's *The Outsider*. Certainly there is ample evidence to support an existentialist reading of the book, but one ought not ignore the other levels of meaning in the novel. Cross Damon's Nietzschean view of the world, his inability to shake, conquer, or comprehend what Wright describes as "that dark part of all lives" (*Native Son* xxv), is blamed on his mother. Cross is aware "intimately and bitterly," he tells us, "that his dread had been his mother's first fateful gift to him. He had been born of her not only physically but emotionally too" (*The Outsider* 17). Thus his nervousness and his high-strung nature (female characteristics) are attributed to his mother's overly religious need to repress/castrate him. "Though she had loved him, she had tainted his budding feelings with a fierce devotion born of her fear of life that had baffled and wounded her" (*The Outsider* 17).

His mother's pain and her lack of self-love prompt Cross to judge himself too harshly. The female character is used to help explain the self-hatred so apparent in the male protagonist. Wright deftly turns the tables in order to imply that the mother, not the son, is incestuous. The female is a *katsi'ka*. Cross Damon apparently believes that his mother blames him for his father's desertion of them:

> She was blaming him somehow for its having gone wrong, confusedly seeking his masculine sympathy for her sexually blighted life! Goddamn her! Had she no sense of shame? This image of his mother's incestuously tinged longings would linger with him for days and he could curse himself for living in a crazy world that he could not set right. (*The Outsider* 21)

Michel Fabre reveals what could account for Wright's apparent ambivalence toward and fear of women. The episodes of violence recounted in *Black Boy* were directed at Wright by the female members of his family (*The Unfinished Quest* 10). In fact, when he was four years old, his mother beat him senseless for setting fire to their house. Wright recalls that for a long time he was chastised whenever he remembered that his mother had come close to killing him (*Black Boy* 13). The violence does not end here. Once when Richard makes a lewd but childishly innocent remark to his grandmother, she violently turns on him. Richard says, "I knew that if I did not get out of her reach she would kill me" (*Black Boy* 51). His mother takes over where his grandmother leaves off. "Come here, you little filthy fool!" his mother shouts. "Come out or I'll beat you within an inch of your life" (*Black Boy* 51). It does not require a Freudian analysis of his childhood experiences to know that such violence from a trusted figure like one's mother can have devastating effects. It is entirely possible that Wright's emotional security is destroyed by the childhood trauma which may have in turn produced an aversion to and hatred of all black women. Hoeveler suggests that Wright eventually understands his conflict with his mother and, in fact projects it into his writing in terms of a self-conscious and increasingly Freudian perspective ("Oedipus Agonistes" 65). Addison Gayle postulates that Wright's

> perceptions of Black women remained on the whole unchanged. Somewhere between poles represented by his mother and grandmother, the universal victim against whom he had to develop intricate defense mechanisms to keep her life from crushing his own and the sternly matriarchy, lay the image with which he was most comfortable. This made it impossible for him to recognize black women—still—as other than abstractions. He was drawn to women who symbolized his mother. But psychologically he was unprepared as an adult to deal with black women whose characteristics bore resemblance to those of the grandmother he was forced to deal with as a child. (*Richard Wright* 106)

Thus far we have seen black female characters cast as castrating matriarchal figures and religious, incestuous figures. Perhaps these unwholesome stereotypes do derive from the memory of the real, physically violent figures who out of fear attempted to crush any section or activity that he could be taken as aggressive in the hostile society where Wright grew up.

The next class of images to consider are the "depreciated sex objects." Gladys and Dot in *The Outsider*, Gladys in *The Long Dream*, Sarah in "Long Black Song," and Bessie in *Native Son* all belong in this category. The depreciated sex objects serve as ego-boosters, tension relievers, tranquilizers. When they have served their purpose, they no longer have any value and are discarded, either physically as Bigger does with Bessie, or emotionally through withdrawal, as Cross does with Gladys. The ideal sex object represents no challenge or threat, emotionally, intellectually, or otherwise. She makes sure that her lover feels as Bigger does in the company of Bessie. "Complete absorption was upon her face. It made him feel alive and gave him a heightened sense of the value of himself" (*Native Son* 135). Bigger felt there were two Bessies: "One a body that he had just had and wanted badly again; the other was in Bessie's face; it asked questions, it bargained and sold the other Bessie to advantage" (135). The Bessie with a face that asks questions is out of synch with the Bessie (body) that Bigger desires, indeed requires. The talking, thinking Bessie precipitates the annihilation of both, because Bigger, feeling threatened, kills her. But before he brutally smashes her head in with a brick, he, in essence, rapes her. "Imperiously driven, he rode roughshod over her whimpering protests, feeling acutely sorry for her as he galloped a frenzied horse down a steep hill in the face of a resisting wind" (*Native Son* 125). The Kierkegaardian epigram "Dread is an alien power which lays hold of an individual, and yet one cannot tear oneself away, nor has a will to do so; for one fears what one desires" (*The Outsider* 1), is as appropriate in *Native Son* as it is in *The Outsider*. The opening chapters of both novels, "Fear" and "Dread," provide evidence of the protagonist's state of mind. Fear and dread are present on both the literal and symbolic levels of the novels—fear and dread of the sex object's alluring power—fear and dread of a senseless world and life one cannot control.

Darwin Turner contends that Bessie symbolizes Bigger's personality. "In Bessie," Turner writes, "he [Bigger] sees a continuation of mental chains. She is still lazily amoral, timid, compliant—in short, the Sambo personality that threatens the existence of the new Bigger. In order to live, Bigger must destroy her, the last link that reminds him of and binds him to his Negroeness" ("The

Outsider: Revision of an Idea" 313). Whether we agree with Turner or see Bessie's potential for becoming a real, thinking, talking, acting person capable of betraying Bigger, thus evoking his sense of fear and dread that leads to murder, is unimportant. The point is that Bessie is never more than a sexual object for the male protagonist, serving either to free his personality as Turner posits or to release his passions and exorcise his dreadful fear.

Female sexuality is problematic for Wright. Addison Gayle reports on an incident from Wright's biography. "Like Bess [note the name], she appealed to him sexually, stirred his passion of growing youth. For this he despised both her and himself" (61). Gayle states that Wright wanted to possess the female body, to own it, control it, to reduce the woman from "powerful, alluring black woman to object, malleable, maneuverable" (61). The woman in question resists his attempt at every turn. Wright says, I hated her then. Then I hated myself for coming to her" (61). The artist's obvious problem with fear and desire is illustrated in the heinous manner by which Bigger disposes of Bessie.

In *The Outsider*, Gladys (Cross Damon's wife) is a cliché image. Damon, whose name phonologically can easily become Daemon, or Demon, is abnormally evil. His oxymoronic name, "Cross Demon" or, as Felgar coins, "crucified demon," indicates his cross between Christ and the devil and may explain Wright's reference to Job: "Mark me, and be astonished, and lay your hands on your mouth" (i). Cross believes he has been duped into marrying Gladys. "In her struggle for legal possession of him, Cross's idea of marriage, her feminine instinct placed him at once in the role of a strong and reliable man and encouraged him to play it" (50). Cross becomes angry when he realizes that Gladys' behavior, so very flattering to him, is a ploy to trap him. Gladys plays perfectly the role ascribed to her. "A registered nurse, quiet, perhaps repressed and with maybe a tendency toward the hysterical, she was soft-spoken, and well-made" (49). Here indeed was a sex object valuable enough to marry, whose value depreciated only with age. Gladys, like Bessie, who bargains and trades her body for the liquor Bigger provides, trades her body for the material objects Cross can provide. Because Cross has never accepted Gladys as anything more than an object for him to possess, when he recognizes her passive-aggressive nature and her ability to manipulate (be deceitful, scheme; still stereotypically female), he realizes "he did not love her" (55), could not love her because she was becoming too much of a real person, too much of a threat. Gladys' value as object is at once depreciated.

Cross first is unfaithful, then abandons her altogether. Gladys, while stereotyped, is not a flat character. "Underneath sex . . . flowed a profounder tide of identity" (51). Once Gladys recognizes that the value of her body has depreciated, she takes extreme and expensive measures to restore the one object with which she can bargain. She has breast implants. Cross, shocked and disgusted by her actions, is apparently unaware of the sexually exploitative way he relates to women. Throughout the novel Cross Damon relates to "woman as body of woman" (28), as the following passage indicates:

> His eyes, trained by habit, followed the jellylike sway of her sloping hips. At once his imagination began a reconstruction of the contour of her body, using the clues of her plump arms, her protruding breast, the gently curving shape of her legs, and the width of her buttocks . . . [he saw her] just as woman, as an image of a body. The girl came toward him now and he looked fully at her; he saw her face: hard, with small reddish eyes; a full, coarsely formed mouth, huge cheekbones that slanted to a stubborn chin, sullen lips . . . an intractable bitch, he thought. (*The Outsider* 24)

Again, the protagonist cannot face the real person, but seeks only to know her body. Gladys, failing to recapture Cross with her body, also becomes an "intractable bitch." Cold, vindictive, and calculating, she refuses to divorce her husband, insisting that he continue to supply her material needs. The added dimension to this depreciated sex object is the Sapphire, evil-blackgirl stereotype.

Dot, as her name implies, has no more significance or substance of character than a mere speck. She represents the amoral teen-aged whore, producer of illegitimate children. Furthermore, she typifies the hysterical depreciated sex object. In *The Outsider* Wright employs the word "hysterical" countless times. The arguments between Dot and Cross are described as "hysterical weeping arguments" (10). Dot and Myrtle, her roommate, are characterized as hysterical (36). Cross wonders, before he actually knows Dot, whether she is "the hysterical breed" (31). Eva acts hysterical (216). Wright is obviously using this word to affirm his acceptance of the emotional stereotyping of women as well as to suggest the psychogenic aspect of the condition of hysteria. Cross comments that "a woman's business is emotion and her trade is carried on in a cash of tears" (44). Lil in *Lawd Today* continues the hysterical tradition. Wright exposes his aversion to tears in the following excerpt: "'Lawd, I wish I was dead,' she sobbed softly. Outside an icy wind swept around the corner of the building, whining and moaning like an idiot in a deep black pit" (224). In *The Long Dream* Emma "wailed and sobs" (66). All the wailing, weeping, hysterical images of women are presented unsympathetically through the icy characterization of Wright, which likens them to idiots.

Cross Damon loves none of the Black women in his life. Turner believes Wright is suggesting "that the male protagonist cannot discover the needed intellectual and spiritual companionship with women of a particular type" (318). Turner should probably say of a particular color, the white prostitute, Jennie, notwithstanding. Wright presents no Black female images capable of sharing an intellectual relationship with his protagonists. Freeing himself from the Black women in his life, Turner tells us that Cross "learns to love only when he meets sensitive, artistic Eva Blount, the first woman who becomes mind as well as body for him" (317). In creating the image of Eva Blount, Wright follows the blueprint for white femininity. Eva (Eve) represents the primal woman—her image is childlike, innocent, pure. Cross "studied her and was amazed to find that she looked even younger without rouge on her lips and cheeks. How did this child—for there was an undeniable childishness about her—fit into his dark broodings . . . ?" (202). This image, while still a stereotype, stands in striking opposition to the Black female image. Eva is not a depreciated sex object. Never referred to as a "bitch" or "whore," morally she is superior even to Cross. When faced with his demonic acts of murder, she commits suicide to escape the reality of her situation.

Sarah in "Long Black Song" is the paragon of amoral sensuality and mindless stupidity. She is not raped and is hardly seduced by the white salesman. Instead, she appears to lead the young man to her bed. She thinks the salesman is "just lika lil boy" (110). When Silas discovers that his wife has been unfaithful, he attempts to whip her, not as one would a child, but "as she had seen him whip a horse" (119). Repeatedly Wright has had the male protagonist blame the female for his troubles. Silas says, "Stabbed in the back by my own blood" (113), referring to his wife. The woman also blames herself. "This was all her fault. Lawd, if anything happens t im its mah blame . . . "

(124). Realizing the deadly consequences of her actions, Sarah offers no explanation; indeed, she appears incapable of understanding her own motivation and can merely utter: "ah didn't mean no harm" (124).

Sarah becomes a depreciated sex object after she sleeps with the salesman. Silas banishes her from his table: "If Yuh wans t eat at mah table yuh gonna keep them white trash bastards out, yuh hear?" (118). Further, he refuses to readmit her unless she submits to a whipping. "Yuh ain comin back in mah house till ah beat yuh!" Silas tells Sarah. But all is lost, for after Silas avenges his "manhood" by killing one white man, he remains to face a rabid mob. His actions, fighting to the death, sending his wife and child to safety, refusing to emerge from the burning house, might be seen as the epitome of gallantry were they not grounded in the paternalistic male chauvinist, materialist perceptions of woman as man's sexual property; and perhaps even more importantly, if Wright had not rendered the sexual encounter between Sarah and the white salesman so ambiguous. Her rape would have called forth a different set of sensibilities. Sarah, stupid, hysterical Sarah, "ran blindly across the fields, crying, 'naw, Gawd!'" (128). Thus the song ends.

In *The Long Dream* Gladys is a prostitute, a depreciated sex object not only because of her trade but due to several other complicated factors involving her color and the way she feels about white people. Fishbelly discovers that Gladys, like Sarah, does not hate or fear whites as he does. Angered by this, he thinks:

> She was a half-white bastard whore who had given birth to a half-white bastard girl child [a boy child was thought more valuable] who was most likely destined to grow up and give birth to yet another half-white bastard girl child who would grow up to be a whore; yet she had never had any trouble with white folks. She was hopeless. Poor little Gladys was just a woman and didn't know. He relished the power he had over her. (190)

The power Gladys has over him ironically resides in the fact that she is half-white. Fishbelly is, as Maybelle, the black-skinned prostitute, so keenly perceives, "a white-struck black fool . . . just hungry for the meat the white man's done made in nigger town!" (158). Fishbelly is, the narrator tells us, "fatally in love with that white world, in love a way that could never be cured" (158). His is the same sick love-hate relationship exposed in "Long Black Song" when Silas declares: "Sho, hire somebody! What yuh think? Ain tha the way the white folks do? Ef yuhs gonna git anywheres yuhs gotta do just like they do" (115). The perils of imitation are clear for both Fishbelly and Silas.

The Long Dream abounds with whores, but with the exception of Gladys, all appear on the periphery of the novel. Gloria, Tyree's whore, while given only surface treatment, is important because of what she represents to Fishbelly:

> Gloria confounded him not only because she had the air of a white woman, but because she acted white. What then did acting white mean? She acted correctly. But what did acting correctly mean? She did not act like a black woman. And how did black women act? He recalled Sam's saying that black people were niggers. . . . Well Gloria was certainly not a nigger. Indeed, she behaved like those white girls in the downtown department stores where he bought neckties. (151)

The narrator tells the reader that Fishbelly had only "blackbelt standards by which to judge Gloria," suggesting that in the white world she would not measure up (151).

Fishbelly loves what he cannot have, and seeks to compensate for it by acquiring an object as close as possible to his ideal. Gladys is the substitute. She asks "'Fish, you really want me?' Her white hands flew across the table and seized hold of him" (191). He wants her but does not fully comprehend his motives. The narrator raises the crucial questions: "was it because she was a shadowy compromise that was white and not white? Was it because she looked white and had to live in the blackbelt with him?" (191). Gladys is a sex object for Fishbelly, but because of her untimely demise in the nightclub fire, we are spared the details of any further depreciation of this female image. The protagonist has been trained how to relate to Black women by his father. Advice from his father has included: "Be hard on these nigger bitches," "A woman's just a woman and the dumbest thing on earth for a man to do is git into trouble about one. When you had one, you done had 'em all" (137). The lesson Fishbelly finds hardest to accept is the one his father deems most important to his son's survival. The father says: "And don't git no screwy ideas about their color. I had 'em white as snow and black as tar and they all the same. The white ones feel just

like the black ones" (137). Despite this admonition, Tyree himself
selects Gloria, the near white object of his adulterous desires.

In the small fictitious town of Clintonville, Mississippi, the
protagonist is limited in his choices of women. On the other hand,
Cross Damon in *The Outsider* has the option of selecting a white
woman and does. Cross says he genuinely loves Eva. Wright delivers
a crushing blow and powerful message to black girls. The black male
protagonists in the works discussed here, when given a choice, select
white over black. Bigger desires Mary Dalton; Fishbelly, the blonde
whose picture he is forced to eat; Cross Damon loves Eva; and alas,
poor Richard, too, chooses white over black. In the world which
birthed him, where he grew and lived learning to hate himself, perhaps
it could not have been otherwise.

Beyond color, a general indictment of women is expressed in
Wright's works. His handling of female characters transcends
stereotype. It is pathological. George Kent states that Wright rejects
the West. Perhaps a more accurate analysis would reveal that Wright
rejects only certain aspects of it, for he embraces wholly the Western
attitudes of male chauvinism. One wonders, in the light of the recent
criticism regarding Black male images in the works of Alice Walker and
Ntozake Shange, how it is that more critics have not mentioned the
images in the works of a writer of the stature of Richard Wright.

References

Aaron, Daniel. "Richard Wright and the Communist Party." *New
    Letters* (Special Issue on Richard Wright), 38 (1971): 170–181.
Alexander, Margaret Walker. "Richard Wright." *New Letters* 38 (1971):
    182–202.
Baker, Houston A. *Long Black Song: Essays in Black American
    Literature and Culture.* Charlottesville: University Press of
    Virginia, 1972.
————. ed. *Twentieth Century Interpretations of "Native Son."*
    Englewood Cliffs, N.J.: Prentice-Hall, 1972.
Baldwin, James. "Ce qui suivivra de Richard Wright." *Prevues* 146
    (1963): 76–79.
————. "Everybody's Protest Novel." *Zéro* (France) 1 (1949): 54–58.
————. "Richard Wright." *Encounter* 16 (1961): 58–60.

————. "The Survival of Richard Wright." *Reporter* 24 (March 16, 1961): 52–55.

————. *Nobody Knows My Name*. New York: Dell, 1961.

————. *Notes of a Native Son*. New York: Dell, 1963.

Bayliss, John F. "*Native Son*: Protest or Psychological Study?" *Negro American Literature Forum* 1 (1967): n.p.

Beauvoir, Simone de. *The Second Sex*. Trans. and ed. H. M. Parshley. New York: Vintage Books, 1974.

Bone, Robert A. *The Negro Novel in America*. New Haven: Yale University Press, 1958.

————. *Richard Wright*. Minneapolis: University of Minnesota Pamphlets on American Writers (no. 74), 1969.

Bosschere, Guy de. "*Fishbelly* de Richard Wright." *Syntheses* 174 (1960): 63–66.

Brignano, Russel C. "Richard Wright: A Bibliography of Secondary Sources." *Studies in Black Literature* 2 (1971): 19–25.

————. *Richard Wright: An Introduction to the Man and His Works*. Pittsburgh: University of Pittsburgh Press, 1970.

Britt, David. "*Native Son*: Watershed of Negro Protest Literature." *Negro American Literature Forum* 1 (1967): n.p.

Brown, Cecil M. "Richard Wright: Complexes and Black Writing Today." *Negro Digest* 18 (1968): 45–50; 78–82.

Brown, Lloyd W. "Stereotypes in Black and White: The Nature of Perception in Wright's *Native Son*." *Black Academy Review* 1 (1970): 35–44.

Bryer, Jackson. "Richard Wright: A Selected Check List of Criticism." *Wisconsin Studies in Contemporary Literature* 1 (1960): 22–33.

Cade, Toni. *The Black Woman*. New York: Signet, 1970.

Cayton, Horace. "Frightened Children of Frightened Parents." *Twice a Year* 12-13 (1945): 262–269.

Christian, Barbara. "Images of Black Women in Afro-American Literature." *Black Feminist Criticism*. New York: Pergamon, 1985.

Cohn, David L. "The Negro Novel: Richard Wright." *Atlantic Monthly* 165 (1940): 659–661.

Creekmore, Hubert. "Social Factors in *Native Son*." *University of Kansas City Review* 7 (1941): 136–143.

Crossman, Richard, ed. *The God That Failed*. New York: Harper and Row, 1963.

Dance, Daryl. "Black Eve or Madonna? A Study of the Antithetical Views of the Mother in Black American Literature." In *Sturdy Black Bridges*, ed. Roseann Bell et al. New York: Doubleday, 1979, pp. 123–132.

Davis, Arthur P. "*The Outsider* as a Novel of Race." *Midwest Journal* 7 (1955-1956): 320–326.

Dickstein, Morris. "Wright, Baldwin, Cleaver." *New Letters* 38 (1971): 117–124.

Ellison, Ralph. "Richard Wright's Blues." *Antioch Review* 5 (1945): 198–211.

Embree, Edwin R. *Thirteen Against the Odds*. New York: Viking, 1944.

Fabre, Michel. "An Interview with Simone de Beauvoir." *Studies in Black Literature* 3 (1970): 3–5.

————. *The Unfinished Quest of Richard Wright*. Trans. Isabel Barzan. New York: William Morrow, 1973.

————. *The World of Richard Wright*. Jackson: University Press of Mississippi, 1985.

Farnsworth, Robert, and Ray Davis, eds. *Richard Wright: Impressions and Perspectives*. Ann Arbor: University Press of Michigan, 1971.

Felgar, Robert. *Richard Wright*. Boston: Twayne, 1980.

Fishburn, Katherine. *Richard Wright's Hero: The Faces of a Rebel-Victim*. Metuchen, N.J.: Scarecrow, 1977.

Ford, J.W. "The Case of Richard Wright." *Daily Worker* 21 (Sept. 5, 1944): 6.

Ford, Nick A. "The Ordeal of Richard Wright." *College English* 15 (1953): 87–94.

French, Warren. *The Social Novel at the End of an Era*. Carbondale: Southern Illinois University Press, 1966.

Gayle, Addison, ed. *Black Expression: Essays by and About Black Americans in the Creative Arts*. New York: Weybright and Talley, 1970.

————. *Richard Wright: Ordeal of a Native Son*. New York: Anchor 1980.

Gibson, Donald B. "Richard Wright: A Bibliographical Essay." *CLA Journal* 12 (1969): 360–365.

————. "Richard Wright and the Tyranny of Convention." *CLA Journal* 12 (1969): 344–357.

————. "Wright's Invisible Native Son." *American Quarterly* 21 (1969): 728-738.

————. "Existentialism in *The Outsider*." *Four Quarters* 7 (1958): 17-26.

————. *Five Black-Writers: Essays on Wright, Ellison, Baldwin, Hughes and LeRoi Jones*. New York: New York University Press, 1972.

Glicksberg, Charles I. "Existentialism in *The Outsider*." *Four Quarters* 7 (1958): 17–26.

Gloster, Hugh M. *Negro Voices in American Fiction*. Chapel Hill: University of North Carolina Press, 1948.

Green, Gerald. "Black to Bigger." *Kenyon Review* 28 (1966): 521–539.

Hakutani, Yoshinobu. *Critical Essays on Richard Wright*. Boston: G.K. Hall, 1982.

Hicks, Granville. "The Power of Richard Wright" (Rev. of *The Long Dream* by Richard Wright). *Saturday Review* 61 (Oct. 18, 1958): 13, 65.

Hodges, John O., "An Apprenticeship to Life and Art: Narrative Design in Wright's *Black Boy*." *CLA Journal* 28 (1985): 415–433.

Hoeveler, Diane Long. "Oedipus Agonistes: Mothers and Sons in Richard Wright's Fiction." *Black American Literature Forum* 12 (1978): 65–68.

Howe, Irving. "Black Boys and Native Sons." *Dissent* 10 (1963): 353–368

Jackson, Blyden. "The Negro's Image of the Universe as Reflected in His Fiction." *CLA Journal* 4 (1960): 22–31.

Jackson, Esther Merle. "The American Negro and the Image of the Absurd." *Phylon* 23 (1962): 359–71.

James, Charles L. "Bigger Thomas in the Seventies: A Twentieth-Century Search for Significance." *English Record* 22 (1971): 6–14.

Kaempffert, Waldemar. "Science in Review—An Author's Mind Plumbed for the Unconscious Factors in the Creation of a Novel." *New York Times* (Sept. 24, 1944): Sec. 4; 11.

Keady, Sylvia H. "Richard Wright's Women Characters and Inequality." *Black American Literature Forum* 10 (1976): 124–128.

Kearns, Edward. "The 'Fate' Section of *Native Son*." *Contemporary Literature* 12 (1971): 146–155.

Kent, George E. "On the Future Study of Richard Wright." *CLA Journal* 7 (1969): 366–370.

———. "Richard Wright: Blackness and the Adventure of Western Culture." *CLA Journal* 12 (1969): 322–343.

King, Mae C. "The Politics of Sexual Stereotypes." *The Black Scholar* 4 (1973): 2–12.

Kinnamon, Kenneth. "*Native Son*: The Personal, Social, and Political Background." *Phylon* 30 (1969): 66–72.

———. *The Emergence of Richard Wright: A Study in Literature and Society*. Urbana: University of Illinois Press, 1972.

Klotman, Phyllis R., and Melville Yancy. "Gift of Double Vision: Possible Political Implications of Richard Wright's 'Self-Consciousness' Thesis." *CLA Journal* 16 (1972): 106–116.

Lawson, Lewis. "Cross Damon: Kierkegaardian Man of Dread." *CLA Journal* 16 (1971): 298–316.

Lehan, Richard. "Existentialism in Recent American Fiction: The Demonic Quest." *Texas Studies in Literature and Language* 1 (1959): 181–202.

Margolies, Edward. *The Art of Richard Wright*. Carbondale: Southern Illinois University Press, 1969.

———. *Native Sons: A Critical Study of Twentieth-Century Negro American Authors*. New York: J.B. Lippincott, 1969.

McCall, Dan. *The Example of Richard Wright*. New York: Harcourt, Brace & World, 1969.

Millett, Kate. *Sexual Politics*. New York: Doubleday, 1970.

Mootry, Maria K. "Bitches, Whores, and Woman Haters: Archetypes and Typologies in the Art of Richard Wright," in *Richard Wright: A Collection of Critical Essays*. Ed. Richard Macksey. Englewood Cliffs, N.J.: Prentice-Hall, 1984.

Reilly, John M. *Lawd Today*: Richard Wright's Experiment in Naturalism." *Studies in Black Literature* 2 (1971): 14–17.

———. "Self-Portraits by Richard Wright." *Colorado Quarterly* 20 (1971): 31–45.

Scott, Nathan A. "The Dark Haunted Tower of Richard Wright." *Graduate Comment* 7 (July 1964): 93–99.

Singh, Amritjit. "Richard Wright's *The Outsider*: Existentialist Exemplar or Critique?" *CLA Journal* 27 (1984): 357–370.

Sprandel, Katherine. "*The Long Dream.*" *New Letters* 38 (1971): 88–96.

Timmerman, John. "Symbolism as a Syndetic Device in Richard Wright's 'Long Black Song'" 16 (1971): 291–297.

Towns, Saundra. "The Black Woman as Whore: Genesis of the Myth." *The Black Position* 3 (1974): 39–59.

Trimmer, Joseph F. *Black American Literature: Notes on the Problem of Definition.* Muncie, Indiana: Ball State Monograph no. 22, 1971.

Turner, Darwin T. "*The Outsider:* Revision of an Idea." *CLA Journal* 12 (1969): 310–321.

Vassilowitch, John. "Erskine Fowler: A Key Freudian Pun in *Savage Holiday.*" *English Language Notes* 18 (1981): 206–208.

Walton, Martha Ballard. "Images of the Black Woman in Afro-American Fiction." *Faculty Research Journal, Texas Southern University* 1 (1976): 66–73.

Watson, Edward A. "Bessie's Blues." *New Letters* 38 (1971): 64–70.

Webb, Constance. *Richard Wright: A Biography.* New York: G. P. Putnam:'s Sons, 1968.

Wertham, Frederic. "An Unconscious Determinant in *Native Son.*" *Journal of Clinical Psychopathology and Psychotherapy* 4 (1944): 111–115.

White, Ralph K. "*Black Boy:* A Value Analysis." *Journal of Abnormal and Social Psychology* 62 (1947): 440–461.

Widmer, Kingsley. "The Existential Darkness: Richard Wright's *The Outsider.*" *Wisconsin Studies in Contemporary Literature* 1 (1960): 13–21.

Williams, John A. *The Most Native of Sons: A Biography of Richard Wright.* Garden City, N.Y.: Doubleday, 1970.

Winslow, Henry F. "Richard Nathaniel Wright: Destroyer and Preserver (1908–1960)." *Crisis* 71 (1962): 149–163, 187.

Wright, Richard. "Long Black Song." *Uncle Tom's Children: Four Novellas.* New York: Harper & Brothers, 1940.

———. *Black Boy.* New York: Harper & Row, 1945.

———. *The Outsider.* New York: Harper & Row, 1953.

———. *The Long Dream.* New York: Doubleday, 1958.

———. *Lawd Today.* New York: Taylor, 1963.

Religious Orthodoxy and Skepticism in Richard Wright's *Uncle Tom's Children* and *Native Son*

Robert L. Douglas

The role of religion in the lives of black people has occasioned some of the most celebrated discussions and debates since blacks became a part of American society. In spite of the fact that slave owners had instructed blacks in a strict Christian doctrine, some anomalies took place in the Christian practice of black people. Not only did the African slaves have their own peculiar ideas about how the deity should be worshipped, but they also wove religious ritual, ceremony, and incantations into the daily fabric of their lives. While these anomalies—once labelled primitive by E. Franklin Frazier and others—are now known to be religious syncretism encompassing African religious phenomena, the masses of blacks have made these practices part of their religious tradition. Therefore, any writing which attempts to portray black life must present some aspect of their particular religious practices. The writings of Richard Wright are no exception.

Since Wright was the first Afro-American writer to spark my interest with his religious allusions, I would like to discuss his use of religious elements in *Uncle Tom's Children* and *Native Son*. The three aspects of black religious life portrayed by Wright and the focus of this inquiry are: (1) the treatment of the minister; (2) the concept of religion or religious worldview; and (3) the use of religious music. Particular stories in several of Wright's short stories reveal concepts in their formative stages which are continued and developed in his novel, *Native Son*. Also, the short stories and novel become excellent instruments for comparing social and aesthetic concepts in Wright's creative practices.

In all of Wright's short stories from the collection *Uncle Tom's Children*, only one of them, "Fire and Cloud," contains the portrait of a minister. In two other stories, "Big Boy Leaves Home" and "Down by the Riverside," Wright portrays minister surrogates, Elder Peters and Elder Murray. Both are equivalent to deacons, and they act as more knowledgeable or wiser community members who are closer to God and who are able to administer God's word, comfort His believers, and engender hope and perseverance. Wright's treatment of the minister, Reverend Taylor, in "Fire and Cloud" is different from his treatment of Reverend Hammond in *Native Son*.

At the beginning of the story, Rev. Taylor is a troubled Southern pastor trying to feed his hungry flock during the Great Depression. At the conclusion he is a determined minister who marches with his congregation, demanding that all their sufferings be alleviated. Rev. Taylor is lied to by a white relief worker, cajoled by the mayor, and threatened by the police chief and a local businessman. He is confronted by his deacon board and insulted by the conniving and envious Deacon Smith. Rev. Taylor empties his pockets to hungry church members, soothes his nervous wife, and cautions his impetuous son. He is kidnapped and beaten by a white mob who tries to force him to call off the march for food. These events change Rev. Taylor from a pastor who had been manipulated by those who wanted control over him and his congregation to a minister who is aware that his power comes from being with his people and not above them. On the morning of the march with his wounds bound he says:

> We's gotta git together, ah know what yo' life is! Ah done felt
> it! It's fire! It's like the fire' that burned me' last night! It's
> sufferin'! It s hell! Ah can't bear this fire erlone! Ah know
> now what t'do! We gotta git close t' one ernother! God
> done'spoke! Gawd done sent' His sign. Now it fer us t ack. . . .
> (178)[1]

Wright fashions a minister whose theology is no longer rooted in endurance and suffering or "pie in the sky" rewards. Rev. Taylor becomes an activist; no less a man of God, but one who realizes that God's chosen people—those who hunger and those who suffer—deserve to have their grievances addressed and ailments healed. As the huge crowd marches in defiance of the mayor and police, Rev. Taylor thinks "This is the way! Gawd ain no lie! He ain no lie! His eyes grew wet with tears . . . he mumbled out loud, exultingly! Freedom belongs t' the strong!" (180).

On the other hand, Rev. Hammond in *Native Son* is condescending and supplicating.[2] Rev. Hammond offers Bigger's mother a theology steeped in suffering and endurance. He believes that man must pay for the original sins of Adam and Eve. He also believes that Adam had begged for forgiveness, and the tenor of his advice to Bigger is that Bigger should do no less. Bigger should not only beg for forgiveness for his violent acts, but he should also do as Rev. Hammond asks: "Son, promise me yuh'll stop hatin' long enuff for Gawd's love to come inter yo heart" (265). Rev. Hammond's meek attitude toward God is manifested in his deference toward whites. When Jan enters the room where Bigger is allowed to receive visitors, Rev. Hammond "took a step backwards, bowed, and said "Good mawnin' suh'" (266). He condescends to a man that is half his age. Rev. Hammond acts in this manner, no doubt, because Jan is white and Rev. Hammond accepts his own inferior social position.

Wright continues his portrayal of Rev. Hammond in *Native Son*. as a meager, obsequious and self-effacing individual. Wright tells his reader that in the presence of Mr. Dalton, "The preacher came forward slowly, hat in hand" and that he proceeded to ingratiate himself. After stating how "sorrowful" he was over Mary Dalton's death, Rev. Hammond supplicates, "Ah knows of yo good work, suh, 'n the likes of this shouldn't come t'yuh" (273).

Wright gives his readers two clearly drawn ministerial types. Rev. Taylor is a strong defender and leader of his people. He cares as much for their physical well being as he does for their souls. Rev. Hammond is weak and ingratiating, beaten by societal forces. All of his energy is directed at saving souls at the expense of the bodies and earthly comforts. Wright, therefore, clothes his skepticism of certain religious beliefs and practices, especially as they pertain to Blacks, in the feelings and attitudes of his protagonist, Bigger.

Although the treatment of the minister types by Wright is individually different, no doubt as types, they share similar characteristics with ministers who are not black. A more distinctive picture of the black minister might have shown his pulpit dramatics or described rhythmic and poetic sermons—none of which appears in either of Wright's works under examination. Thus, Wright's minister types are not as peculiar to blacks as is his presentation of the black religious worldview and black religious music.

At the root of the religious worldview of the black masses is the perception of God in the most elemental and literal levels. Such practices are often characterized as child-like and unsophisticated. Dr. Benjamin E. Mays in his classic study, *The Negro's God as Reflected in His Literature*, demonstrated that blacks' belief in God assumes an orthodox point of view from an Old Testament orientation (p. 14).[3] Mays also contends that blacks place special emphasis upon "the magical, spectral, partial, revengeful and anthropomorphic nature of God" (14).

Dr. Mays says that the black religious worldview is "compensatory when used or developed to support a shallow pragmatism" (16). A religious belief becomes true when it satisfies a desire, if it uplifts and consoles even though the belief does not fit observed facts. Mays explains these assertions by saying:

> A dependent mother who prays to [God] twice daily asking him to bless her sons, preserve their lives, and cause them to prosper (thinking her task is done after she prays) is typical of an idea of God that supports such pragmatism. (14)

As an example of the religious anomalies of blacks, such a worldview influences the mother's behavior: "it leads her to pray; it helps her to feel better; it saves her from worry, and it enables her to sleep at night" (14).

In Wright's short story "Big Boy Leaves Home," Elder Peters is summoned to the Morrison home for advice. Elder Peters invokes "Gawd's" name more than once to assure his friends that he speaks with a heavenly endowed wisdom (*Children* 39). Elder Murray in "Down by the Riverside" stops by Mann and Lula's home on his way to higher ground from the surging flood waters, to see if he can assist them in any way, but before he leaves, he leads them in prayer. He begins,

> Lawd Gawd almighty in Heaven, we a-bowin be fo yah once ergin, humble in yo sight, a-pleadin fer fergiveness n mercy! Hear us today, Lawd, Hear us today if yah ain never heard us befo! We needs yah now t help us n guide us! (62)

After enumerating specific needs and reminding "Gawd" to soften the hard hearts of white folks, Elder Murray ends his prayer with the old spiritual "Down by the Riverside." Wright creates what Dr. Mays refers to as a "constructive development of the idea of God to support a growing consciousness of needed social adjustment" (*Negro's God* 16). Rev. Taylor assumes that "Gawd intended that his torment and suffering was a sign for his social involvement" (*Children* 156). Earlier Rev. Taylor assured the conniving Deacon Smith that:

> Gawd Almighty Himself put me here. Ahm stayin till He says fer me t' ! Yuh been schemin to git me out', but yuh can't do it this way! It ain' right n Gawd know it ain! Yeah, if my folks marches in the mawnin ahm marchin wid em! (157)

According to Dr. Mays, no people believe in the partiality or the ultimate justice of God more than blacks. This New Testament concept of love, justice, and fairness is illustrated by Wright as Rev. Taylor consoles himself as he struggles to get home after being beaten by a white mob. He says:

> Someday theys gonna burn! Somday theys gonna burn in Gawd Almighty's fire! How come they make us suffer so? Gawd knows that ain' right! He made the earth fer us' all. He ain tol no' lie when He put us in this worl an said be fruitful n multiply . . . Gawd ef yuh gimme the strength Ah'll tear this ol' buildin down! ear ut down, Lawd! Tear ut down like ol' Sampson tore the temple down! Lawd, tell me what t do! Speak to me, Lawd! (167)

For Rev. Taylor, Wright's representative of the common black believer, the bible is a sacred treatise of what to believe and how to act. Biblical messages are not symbols or allegory; the bible is fundamental and literal.

Dr. Mays states that the black view of God as it is reflected through black literature can be divided into three categories and time periods. The first, the other-worldly or the orthodox treatment with its compensatory pragmatism, appeared during slavery. The second, God's concern for black social and psychological needs, can be placed between the failure of Reconstruction and the First World War. The third, the tendency to abandon the idea of God as a useful agent of social change,

appears more often in black literature after the First World War. Dr.
Mays contends that this disillusionment was caused by the fact that the
promise of greater social freedom did not materialize as many hoped
following the War. According to Dr. Mays none of the three religious
views ever existed solely by itself, and although his study does not go
beyond 1937, much about this theory remains relevant. The skepticism
and cynicism evident in Wright may be seen as falling into Mays' third
category. To quote Dr. Mays, "for recent writers to consider the idea of
God as useless is an effort to reconstruct the world socially" (251).

In *Native Son*, Wright shows religious doubt, frustration, and
cynicism in a most blatant manner as Wright's protagonist expresses
the frustration born out of waiting for God to solve his problem. When
Max questions Bigger about his religious beliefs, Bigger tells him, "I
didn't like it. There was nothing in it" (329). Bigger feels that "church-
going" is a delusion and a way for keeping poor people happy while
they remain poor. He expresses his doubts about church and the
promises of religion.

> Aw, all they did was sing and shout and pray all the time. And
> it didn't get em nothing. All the colored folks do that, but it
> don't get'em nothing. The white folks got everything. (329)

Bigger also states that he never felt happy in church nor did he
want to be because, "nothing but poor folks get happy in church"
(329). Bigger's skepticism about the social value of church borders on
an astute political awareness. He refuses to be caught up in the
traditional religious orthodoxy of the heaven-or-hell alternative or the
idea that one would receive a reward for his suffering after his death. He
says,

> I want to be happy in this world, not out of it. I did't want that
> kind of happiness. The white folks like for us to be religious,
> then they can do what they want to with us. (329)

If Dr. Mays is correct that the black tends to move beyond God as a
catalytic social agent and that black writers reflect this change through
their art, then Wright's skepticism and his incipient agnosticism
blossom in his characterization of Bigger Thomas. In fact, Bigger is
portrayed as a developing atheist. The more Rev. Hammond attempts
to awaken in Bigger a sense of guilt and forgiveness, the more Bigger

rejects the preacher and his theology. Later, as Rev. Hammond tries to assure Bigger that he would meet his mother in the "great bye and bye," Bigger's atheistic feelings became more evident. The reader is told that, "Something screamed deep down in [Bigger] that it was a lie, that seeing [his mother] after they killed him would never be" (278). After listening to Rev. Hammond's orthodox view of creation—man's sinful place in it and how Jesus was sent to save man—Bigger thought about how "he had killed within himself the preacher's haunting picture of life even before he had killed Mary" (264). Also, Bigger felt that "to those who wanted to kill him he was not human, not included in that picture of creation" (264).

Wright prepares his reader for Bigger's involvement with the death of Mary Dalton and Bessie as well as the inevitable consequences by showing the reader the brutality of the life that Bigger was forced to survive and the situations that fired Bigger's doubts. After allowing Rev. Hammond to put a cross around his neck, Bigger comes out of the Dalton home, where he is taken for further questioning; and he sees a burning cross placed there by the Ku Klux Klan. His thoughts become an insight into his cynicism. "He had a cross of salvation round his throat and they were burning one to tell him that they hated him" (313). Bigger felt that he had been trapped by the preacher who was also trapped in a religion that could not save either of them.

Wright uses church music or spirituals to enhance his stories and to express the tribulation or jubilation of his characters. Wright also uses religious music as a structural element to tie events together and to give his stories an aesthetic form.

There is at least one religious song of significance in each of Wright's short stories. In the first, "Big Boy Leaves Home" Wright employs the old spiritual "Glory Train" as a metaphorical device with ironic impact. As the story begins, Big Boy, Bobo, Buck, and Lester, the central characters, express their jubilation and youthful desire to escape their boring environment with an old religious hymn—"Dis train bound fo glory, dis train, oh hallelujah." The spontaneous burst into song was prompted by the sound of the northbound train. The song "Glory Train" is an ironic foreshadowing of the terrible events that follow. The train to glory or to freedom in Big Boy's case is a large freight truck carrying southern products to a Chicago market.

The second story in Wright's collection, entitled "Down by the Riverside," and his fifth one, "Bright and Morning Star," make a direct use of the spirituals, beginning with their titles. The music in each story heightens the sense of drama either by emphasis or irony and sometimes by both. In the second story, a flood threatens the household of the central characters. But when nature's awesome force is abated, the blacks still have to contend with the flood of violence from the white community. Wright uses the content of the song "Down by the Riverside" to give ironic import to the story. The words, which the blacks sing with religious intensity, are "Ahm gonna lay down mah sword and sheel," and "Ah ain gonna study war no mo" (63). It is obvious that the white community has no such intentions. Whites force the blacks to labor under perilous conditions on the levee and and shoot them if they refuse. The refrain "Ah ain gonna study war no mo" becomes a haunting backdrop, when Mann, the protagonist, who had asked for the prayer and the song earlier, is shot trying to escape vigilante law for having defended himself and his family. The reader is told that his body rolls down to the river's edge—"to study war no mo," and Wright has created a masterful display of literary metaphor and irony.

Wright combines religious ecstasy with earthly desires, forlorn dreams, and sexual delight in "Long Black Song." The female protagonist, Sarah had married for convenience. Caught in her earthly desires and forlorn longing for the man she loved, Sarah was awakened from her "long black song" by a white salesman who became the surrogate partner of her sexual desires.

Wright creatively and somewhat unconventionally intermingles the religious ecstasy experienced by Sarah with her emotional response at a more mundane level. The reader is told that:

> Her body caught in the ringing coil of music
> > (when the trumpet of the Lord shall sound . . .)
> She rose on circling waves of white bright days and dark black
> > nights.
> > (. . . time shall be no more . . .)
> Higher and higher she mounted.
> > (and the morning breaks . . .)
> Earth fell far behind, forgotten
> > (. . . eternal, bright and fair . . .)
> Echo after echo sounded
> > (when the saved of the earth shall gather . . .)
> Her blood surged like the long gladness of summer.

   (. . . over the other shore . . .)
Her blood ebbed like the deep dream of sleep in winter.
   (and when the roll is called up yonder . . .)
She gave up, holding her breath,
   (I'll be there . . .)   (110)

Misreading Sarah's response to the music, the white salesman began to confront her sexually. Her protestations fell on deaf ears as the salesman relentlessly pursued her. The reader is told that Sarah rejected her encounter because it was with a white man rather than because it was wrong or undesirable. "Long Black Song" has many symbolic implications, among them are rhythmic feelings of primal desires, a spiritual song born of suffering, the age old insult felt by Silas when he fathoms his wife's unfaithfulness, or the final response of a black man who decides to give his life in defense of an injured and an oppressed people who have suffered such abuses too long.

Wright also uses religious songs to give solace and spiritual strength so that his characters might endure. The protagonist in "Bright and Morning Star" like Sarah, is a woman, but she is older and a mother of two grown sons. She is also dedicated and faithful. She states that she had learned the "songs" as a child as "slow strains (floating) from her mother's lips," and their meaning from the hardship in her own life; but more "she has poured the yearnings of her life into the songs, feeling buoyed with faith beyond the World" (184).

However, to convey the complexity of black life through richly textured literary genre, Wright uses black music in *Native Son* as symbolism and metaphor. The mention of a grave in her first song can be taken as a foreshadowing device of the death of Bigger's victims and himself. After he kills Mary and Bessie, Bigger hears the old slave spiritual "Steal Away to Jesus" as he is attempting his own flight to freedom.

Wright's waxing and waning between religious orthodoxy and skepticism signifies his continuing attempt to come to grips with Christian doctrine. His treatment of one aspect of black religious life in one narrative may have its opposite portrayal in another, i.e., Ministers Hammond and Taylor. Or the religious strength and catharsis embedded in religious music for an older black woman may become the religious ecstasy that can be twisted into sexual passion for a younger one. Perplexed about the values of Christianity as a means of black salvation and liberation, not knowing how it can be of value to black people or if it can be, Wright is torn between religious orthodoxy and skepticism.

Notes

1. Richard Wright, *Uncle Tom's Children* (New York: Harper & Row Publishers, 1965), 178. All citations from this collection are hereafter marked by page numbers in parentheses following the mention of same.
2. Richard Wright, *Native Son* (New York: Harper & Row Publishers, 1966), 265. All citations from this novel are hereafter marked by page numbers in parentheses following mention of same.
3. Benjamin Mays, *The Negro's God as Reflected in His Literature* (New York: Russell & Russell, 1938), 14. All citations from this book are hereafter marked by page numbers in parentheses following mention of same.

Richard Wright's Beckoning Descent and Ascent

Marjorie Smelstor

Though Richard Wright produced three books frequently labeled autobiographical—*Native Son* (1940), *Black Boy* (1945), and *American Hunger* (1977)—only the last two are true autobiographies. James Olney points out that "*Native Son* is not an autobiography because in the making of it memory does not reach back into an historical, personal past, back down the Heraclitean stream, to retrace a lifetime, the course of life."[1] But I do not agree with Olney's assertion that "only *Black Boy* does that" [retraces a lifetime] because both *Black Boy* and *American Hunger* retrace the lifetime of Richard Wright, using memory to recreate the experience of going back in order to go forward. This reliance upon memory shapes the autobiographer's portrait, resulting in both self-definition and self-renewal in the way that William Carlos Williams describes in *Paterson*:

> The descent beckons
> >   as the ascent beckoned
> > >   memory is a kind
> > of accomplishment
> >   a sort of renewal
> > >   even
> >   an initiation, since the spaces it opens are new
> >   places
> > >   inhabited by hordes
> > > >   heretofore unrealized . . . [2]

Furthermore, it is important to consider these two books of initiation as one book, which, in fact, is what Richard Wright intended.

Instead of two volumes, the first covering Wright's experiences in Chicago up to 1927 and the second chronicling the next decade of his life, Wright had planned a combined volume, entitled *American Hunger*, though he commented in a letter that he thought *Black Hunger* "would be a better title."[3] The reason for publishing the two volumes separately is unclear. It may have been the decision of the Book-of-the-Month Club, which accepted the autobiography on the condition that it include only Wright's experiences in the South. Or it may have been the decision of Edward Aswell, Wright's editor at Harper's and his loyal advisor. As early as January 1944 Aswell suggested Wright publish the two pieces separately, and though Wright apparently agreed to do so at the time, it is not clear if the actual decision was Wright's, Aswell's, or the Book-of-the-Month Club's editors.[4]

We do not know who finally made the publishing decision, but we do know that Wright wrote the piece as a whole, even though he was prepared to have "a section or two here and there" pulled out, as he wrote in a letter to Paul Reynolds in December 1943, the same letter in which he commented on the title *Black Hunger*. Was he prepared to have such a big section—the equivalent of an entire volume—pulled out? That is still not clear.

Just as we know that Wright conceived of the work as a whole piece, so we know that he intended a self-portrait that would ultimately be not a pleasant, nostalgic trip into the past but rather a painful wrestling with the self. In "The Birth of Black Boy," which appeared in the *New York Post* on November 30, 1944, he contrasted writing about his life with speaking about it, which he did at Fisk University in 1942 when he gave a lecture about his formative years:

> The real hard terror of writing like this came when I found that writing of one's life was vastly different from speaking of it. I was rendering a close and emotionally connected account of my experience and the ease I had had in speaking from notes at Fisk would not come again. I found that to tell the truth is the hardest thing on earth, harder than fighting in a war, harder than taking part in a revolution. If you try it you will find that at times sweat will break upon you. You will find that even if you succeed in discounting the attitudes of others to you and your life, you must wrestle with yourself most of all, fight with yourself; for there will surge up in you a strong desire to alter facts, to dress up your feelings. You'll find that there are many

things that you don't want to admit about yourself and others. As your record shapes itself an awed wonder haunts you. And yet there is no more exciting an adventure than trying to be honest in this way. The clean, strong feeling that sweeps you when you've done it makes you know that.[5]

These are harsh words, reminiscent of an attitude toward writing that an Ernest Hemingway or some other equally hardboiled author might articulate. How, then, to explain the fact that *Black Boy*, the book about which Wright was actually writing in this article, represents this attitude less than *American Hunger*, which seems like a much "sweatier" book than *Black Boy?* Michel Fabre points out that in *Black Boy* Wright's explanatory comment "does not really blend with the story's dialogue, its descriptions, its action, or its lyrical outbursts; it is a reflexive voice which enables the reader to gauge the passage of the author's life and the ensuing change in his perspective."[6] This "meditation," as Fabre describes it, concludes with five pages that have been criticized for being too lyrical, too optimistic, too overwritten. In reality, the pages were added hastily and, though Fabre sees them and the last paragraph in particular as "a nearly mystical expression of hopeful potentialities," they are actually sophomoric efforts at closure. How do we evaluate this lack of "blend," to use Fabre's term? How do we approach this apparent discrepancy between an author's stated intention and its embodiment in two works, two works that are quite different in tone?

How do we handle the question of poetry versus polemic, the first being characteristic of *Black Boy* and the second of *American Hunger?* Since we know that both books were originally one book, do we conclude that Wright began as a poet and ended as a polemicist?

As with most important questions, these are finally unanswerable. But they are challenging nonetheless, forcing us to look more closely at these self-portraits, reminding us that labels such as "slave narrative tradition" do not always explain the dynamics in a work, especially if the work is a book which really doesn't exist: *Black Hunger*. This non-book is also paradoxical in another way, for, in its two volumes, it is both Aristotelian and Longinian, a blend that poses tremendous problems for the literary critic.[7] On the one hand, both *Black Boy* and *American Hunger* are informed by an Aristotelian belief in *product*— that is, a commitment to the unities, a detachment from the reader, a reliance upon predictable conventions. But the books are also informed by an opposite impulse, a Longinian emphasis upon *process* that necessarily means a reliance upon the continuous present, unpredictability, involvement of the reader. Both the Aristotelian and Longinian approaches to literature, the one being aesthetic and the other psychological, are present in Wright's autobiographies. As a result, the two books are both frustrating and tantalizing, annoying us, for instance, with Wright's apparent need to end *Black Boy* neatly and yet tantalizing us with the suggestion that this facile ending is also a lyrical paean to the unfinished quality of the self, a recognition that process, with its belief in perpetual, unending motion, is the only appropriate way to "end" the product.

My distinction between process and product, as it is applied to Richard Wright, resembles Elizabeth Schultz's contrast between testimonial and blues autobiographies. Among the former she includes Frederick Douglass and W. E. B. DuBois, writers whom she believes are "concerned with objectification and development of a specific conviction." Blues autobiographers, by contrast, are "concerned with the process of discovering meaning, a process synonymous with the discovery of consciousness, with the reader implicitly being engaged in this process." Referring to Ralph Ellison's essay on *Black Boy*, she persuasively shows how Wright's book, as well as the self-portraits by Zora Neale Hurston and Claude McKay, resembles blues, based on the concept of the *solo*, but expanding that voice of the single individual to include the tone of the tribe.

Schultz also considers the fact that blues autobiographers sometimes write their life stories "in supplements" that differ from the revised versions that testimonial autobiographers produce. While Douglass and DuBois write their versions "conclusively," says Schultz, Anne Moody, Maya Angelou, and Langston Hughes, representative blues autobiographers, write volumes that are "only a portion of an extensive manuscript which is ever in process."[8] Like critics Sidonie Smith and Roger Rosenblatt,[9] Elizabeth Schultz points to the cyclical quality of blues autobiographies, self-portraits which are the songs of wandering troubadours.

I do not disagree with Schultz's distinction between testimonial and blues autobiographies; in many ways this distinction parallels my own contrast between Aristotelian and Longinian life stories. I do question, however, the implication that Wright's *Black Boy* is simply a blues autobiography. It is much more than that. It is blues and testimonial;

it is Aristotelian and Longinian; it is product and process. It is *Black Boy* and *American Hunger*. This "descent beckons"—it beckons us to consider its complexities, not its deceptive neatness.

BLACK BOY

Chapter 1 of *Black Boy* is a microcosm of the tantalizing frustration that is Richard Wright's autobiography. It is also, as Albert Stone points out, "as neat a synecdoche as can probably be found in the history of modern American autobiography."[10] Structurally and thematically, it appears to be less a well-ordered, unified record—*A Record of Childhood and Youth*, as the subtitle of the book tells us—than a series of discrete images suggesting the struggle of growing up and, specifically, growing up as a black boy in the South. Though it opens with a line that is straightforward and traditional enough ("One winter morning in the long-ago, four-year-old days of my life"), this predictable announcement is followed by a *mélange* of scenarios, unified by the fact that they all relate to the experience of childhood but disconnected by the fact that these scenarios are left to speak for themselves, without transitions or commentaries. In this respect, they are almost like Lillian Hellman's cameos in *Pentimento*: portraits she has painted on her literary canvas.

The first image is fire, the fire Richard sets out of boredom. From there we move to the image of the murdered kitten, another consequence of Richard's mood, this one being anger at and revenge toward his father. Other images follow: peeking at people in the outhouse, eating Sunday dinner with the preacher, begging for money in the saloon, and other glimpses of Richard's early years. The camera pans over all this, providing a panoramic view of these experiences but never offering any close-ups or any explanatory comments.

Even the narrative voice shifts, making us wonder who this autobiographical character truly is. As with Maya Angelou, the varying voices are disconcerting, a challenge to the reader's ear. Is the speaker assuming the role of journalist, reporting recollected events with clarity and objectivity so that the autobiography is truly *A Record of Childhood and Youth*? After all, we are given, straightforwardly and directly, a chronicle of the fire that destroys the house, the kitten whose murder angers the parents, the saloon scenes that show a hungry, drunken child. We read these sections much as we would read a newspaper article reporting on the day's events.

Or is the narrator really a poet, giving us Whitmanesque catalogs of natural events?

> There was the delight I caught in seeing long straight rows of red and green vegetables stretching away in the sun to the bright horizon.
> There was the faint, cool kiss of sensuality when dew came on to my cheeks and shins as I ran down the wet green garden paths in the early morning.
> There was the vague sense of the infinite as I looked down upon the yellow, dreaming waters of the Mississippi River from the verdant bluffs of Natchez.[11]

Is this a lyrical voice of a young wordsmith, a suggestion that we're not reading the product of a journalist so much as we're watching the evolution of the artist? Is this narrator a Joycean, a poet who is giving us his own version of the portrait of the artist as a young man?[12]

Or perhaps we're hearing the preacher, the didactic voice of the orator who is inclined to sermonizing and commentary. Just as this voice, in a later chapter, will comment on his mother's suffering as a "symbol [of] the meaningless pain and the endless suffering," so does it now suggest the symbolism of his father, seen a quarter of a century after the poet and reporter have provided images and scenes of childhood. This adult vision sees the father as representing alienation, the fractured relationship of father and son, past and future:

> ". . . when I tried to talk to him I realized that, though ties of blood made us kin, though I could see a shadow of my face in his face, though there was an echo of my voice in his voice, we were forever strangers, speaking a different language, living on vastly distant planes of reality." (42)

The preacher who is now speaking no longer reports or rhapsodizes; he no longer *shows* us childhood. He *tells* us: "I forgave him and pitied him. . . ."

Moving from scene to scene, adjusting our ears to different voices, we appear to be in the midst of an autobiography that is Longinian, concerned with the process of creating the self in all its chameleon-like, unpredictable, unfinished dimensions. We are given the impression, as we are in all works in which process is more important than product, that the autobiography is being created before our eyes.

But this is actually sleight of hand, for Chapter 1 of *Black Boy*, and, in fact, the entire autobiography, is a carefully constructed product with no totally unpredictable white rabbits jumping out of hats. Structurally, for instance, the first chapter may give the appearance of an experimental prose poem, but it is actually constructed in a traditional way of having the opening and closing sections neatly frame the entire chapter. We begin with the adult voice, and we end with the adult voice. We begin with the startling depiction of fire and we end with two other variations on this fire image: the bright fire blazing in the grate at the home of Richard's father and the reference to the city of "burning arms."

Thematically, each image is also related, not just by the general topic of childhood experiences but by the more specifically autobiographical concern with education. Each scene reveals the ways in which the young Richard learns about himself and the society from which he will always be separate. From the early fire episode, for instance, he begins to understand the desire for invisibility of Ralph Ellison's protagonist. From the murdered kitten episode, he sees the power of destruction: at someone or something's expense, another can feel victory, just as the young Richard tasted what he called his "first triumph" over his father.

He is also educated by mentors, some positive and some negative. The coal man teaches him numbers and his mother teaches him words, tools that can ultimately liberate him. But Miss Simon teaches him to be and use a blotter—to soak up the legalistic requirements of a society that forbids questions and discourages creativity. She "killed something" in him, the narrator recalls, just as the adults in the bar who had forced the young boy to beg for pennies and become a childhood drunk also killed something in him: his dignity. When his father duplicates that kind of education, offering his hungry child a nickel, the conflict in Richard's education becomes apparent: Should he learn to be a "fool," as his father warned his mother ("Don't teach him to be a fool")? Should he be foolish enough to go hungry rather than give up his dignity and humanity? Or should he learn to be self-determining, even if that means living with physical and spiritual emptiness?

Thematically and structurally, these questions are answered in Chapter 1 of *Black Boy*. Unlike autobiographies which are more Longinian than Aristotelian, more comfortable with unanswered questions than settled solutions, Wright's self-portrait, from this first chapter of *Black Boy* to the last pages of *American Hunger*, asserts an answer to the question of creating the self: purification comes from destruction. The fire does destroy the home in the opening pages of *Black Boy*, but it also illuminates the relationship between father and son, thus creating a new kind of freedom for Richard Wright. He concludes the chapter by saying that his father's face was "lit by the dancing flames" and that the illumination was "so vivid and strong" that he could almost reach out and touch it. Most importantly, he says that this illuminated image "possessed some vital meaning" which always eluded him. But the elusive image *does* become meaningful; it becomes meaningful because Wright makes meaning out of it by making an autobiography. He can thus say in the last paragraph—after commenting on the meaning that had eluded him—that he and his father had chosen the same path, the city, but had become different persons, the father having become "a black peasant whose life had been hopelessly snarled in the city" and the son having been lifted up by that same city and "borne . . . toward alien and undreamed-of shores of knowing." The father had remained, as Wright notes, "animalistic," whereas the son had added knowledge to his more base impulses of hunger and fear. The autobiographer can therefore say that he forgave and pitied his father, a very different attitude from the child's feeling of "deep biological bitterness."

This conclusion to Chapter 1 seems like a lovely, poetic denouement, a simple terminus to a journey to the North and to the inner core of the self. But it is *too* lovely and simple for an autobiographer who uses Job as his epilogue:

> They meet with darkness in the daytime
> And they grope at noonday as in the night.

More importantly, it is too simple for a man, an educated man, who has learned that the process of becoming educated and the place where that happens—"alien and undreamed-of shores of knowing"—are neither lovely nor poetic. On the contrary, Richard Wright's physical and psychological journey, which, we must remember, has already occurred and is informing his description of his father, has taught him that knowledge reveals not truth, beauty, and goodness, but lies, ugliness, and evil. As Richard said to the principal who wanted him to read a valedictory speech which he, the principal, had written instead of one that Richard wrote, "I want to learn . . . but there are some things I don't want to know." He does not want to know the lies that subjugate blacks, the ugliness that forces blacks to live in hunger and fear, the evil that prevents blacks from being conscious of possibilities. Through "rejection, rebellion, and aggression," words he uses at the end of *Black Boy* to describe his youthful frustrations and his adolescent responses, he substitutes this learning for knowledge.

This substitution is the factor that makes *Black Boy* both an Aristotelian and Longinian autobiography. The book proceeds through predictable, chronological sequence, even to the point of mentioning years and dates—for example, "With almost seventeen years of baffled living behind me, I faced the world in 1925." Our expectations are generally fulfilled. For instance, when we expect Richard to be conned into fighting his friend Henderson to make money for himself and to make laughter for the white men, that is precisely what happens. When we expect him to resist the seduction by Bess, the seventeen-year-old daughter of his landlord in Memphis, that is exactly what he does. When we expect the white men in the optician's shop to harass and frighten the young black apprentice, that is what they do.

All this predictability, furthermore, is delivered in a clear, balanced fashion. We have a book that, like its first, microcosmic chapter, is organized clearly, that proceeds systematically, that hardly ever allows "the qualities of subconscious association" to take the lead. We feel secure in the hands of a conscious—in fact, self-conscious—storyteller, and as a result we respond in the detached, admiring way that spectators view the smooth unraveling of an aesthetic product. Like a well-made play, *Black Boy* gives us a *record* of childhood and youth.

But just as Elizabeth Schultz sees this book as blues and not testimonial, so I see it as more than an autobiographical product. The shifting voices we hear in the first chapter contribute to the tentative identity of the narrator, and those voices continue to fluctuate throughout the book. The poetic catalogues inserted in the record, plus the poetic conclusions of the first and last chapter, also add to the Longinian qualities of the self-portrait. But the most telling quality of this autobiography and its concern with the process of creating the self

as opposed to the finished product is the fact that the subtitle of this
book should really be the title of Joyce's *kunstleroman*. This book is
really a portrait of the artist as a young man, with the emphasis upon
young—hence naive, unfinished, immature.

This young man is yearning and learning to be an artist. He trains
himself to hear the "cryptic tongues" and let them reveal "their coded
meanings," as he says in the first chapter. And in the next chapter,
when he notes that "the days and hours began to speak now with a
clearer tongue [with] a sharp meaning of their own," he is chronicling
his growth as both a man and as an artist. He publishes a story entitled
"The Voodoo of Hell's Half-Acre," and he reads Mencken, Sinclair
Lewis, and Dreiser, thus serving his apprenticeship as a writer. He is
learning about creation, about making meaning of a meaningless world
and the multiple selves that make up the self. As an artist, he comes to
see the futility of changing the word or even of altering "one's
relationship to one's environment," but he does begin to see what he
must do: go north "precisely to change." If he cannot change the
external world of ugliness, lies, and evil, he can change his internal
world. But the artist is still a young man. He recognizes his
immaturity in various events, including his near-seduction by Bess and
his actual collaboration in a scam operation: "Last night I had found a
naive girl. This morning I had been a naive boy." But he does not yet
recognize his youth in his writing. He does not see the qualitative
difference between his controlled prose, which is usually poetic and
lyrical, spelling out, as he puts it, "magical possibilities" (81), and his
uncontrolled sentimentality, evidenced in the last pages of *Black Boy*.
The last sentence of the book is a particularly good example of the
artist as a young man, and it contrasts with the last sentence of the first
chapter, which is the effort of the artist as a maturing creator:

> With ever watchful eyes and bearing scars, visible and
> invisible, I headed North, full of a hazy notion that life could
> be lived with dignity, that the personalities of others should
> not be violated, that men should be able to confront other men
> without fear or shame, and that if men were lucky in their living
> on earth they might win some redeeming meaning for their
> having struggled and suffered here beneath the stars. (285)

In this paean of purple prose we hear youth, unbridled idealism,
uncontrolled diction. Absent is the ominous ambiguity of the final

sentence of Chapter 1, the sentence written from the perspective of "a quarter of a century" of purgation:

> From far beyond the horizons that bound this bleak plantation there had come to me through my living the knowledge that my father was a black peasant who had gone to the city seeking life, but who had failed in the city; a black peasant whose life had been hopelessly snarled in the city, and who had at last fled the city—that same city which had lifted me in its burning arms and borne me toward alien and undreamed-of shores of knowing. (43)

Among many significant qualities in this passage is the texture of the words *knowledge* and *knowing*, a texture we only understand after we've taken the journey, with Richard, to the end of the book, which, like Eliot's journey, is actually the beginning, since "in the end is my beginning."

The artist as a young man was obsessed with these words. Wondering about his mysterious "uncle," he mused that he "was destined never to know, not even in all the years that followed." Concerned about his "lopsided" personality, he noted that his "knowledge of feeling was far greater than . . . [his] knowledge of fact." Angry at his school principal, he announced that he wanted to learn but that there were some things he didn't "want to know." And caught up in the idea of being an artist, but naively "running more away from something than toward something," he confidently proclaimed and youthfully repeated—too confidently and too youthfully—his knowledge in the last pages of the autobiography:

> The face of the South that I had *known* was hostile and forbidding, and yet out of all the conflicts and the curses, the blows and the anger, the tension and the terror, I had somehow gotten the idea that life could be different, could be lived in a fuller and richer manner. . . . The external world of whites and blacks, which was the only world that I had ever *known*, surely had not evoked in me any belief in myself. . . . Well, the white South had never *known* me—never *known* what I thought, what I felt. . . . Not only had the southern whites not *known* me, but, more important still, as I had lived in the South I had not had the chance to learn who I was. . . . I was leaving the South to fling myself into the *unknown*, to meet other situations that

would perhaps elicit from me other responses. (281–284; emphasis added)

Unlike the voice at the end of Chapter 1 that speaks of knowledge and knowing as a complex product and process, replete with "alien and undreamed-of shores," the other voices simplify and reduce, typical actions of youth. The artist as a young man who flings himself into the "unknown" does not yet see the fires that are waiting to purge him. He does not yet realize that the scars, "visible and invisible," he has at the age of eighteen are nothing compared with the scars he will have only ten years later when he sees the black peasant who is his father and has an epiphany that arises from and adds to his complicated knowledge:

> . . . I was overwhelmed to realize that he could never understand me or the scalding experiences that had swept me beyond his life and into an area of living that he could never know. I stood before him, poised, my mind aching as it embraced the simple nakedness of his life, feeling how completely his soul was imprisoned by the slow flow of the seasons, by wind and rain and sun, how fastened were his memories to a crude and raw past, how chained were his actions and emotions to the direct, animalistic impulses of his withering body. . . . (42–43)

The voice in this passage sees not only his father but also himself, his other, younger self, imprisoned and chained by impulses. Sometimes it was the impulse to flee, which he responded to by running from Jackson to Memphis to Chicago. Sometimes it was the impulse to fear, whether the object of the fear was beatings from Granny, Aunt Addie, or Uncle Tom, or the rejection that might come from any white man who expected invisibility from blacks. Still other times it was the impulse to feel ("my knowledge of feeling was far greater than my knowledge of fact," he wrote about his beginning at Jim Hill public school). Whatever the impulse, the artist as a young man was always impulsive and often compulsive.

The artist as a not-so-young man, however, is less impulsive and compulsive and more reflective. He has learned to do more than merely *see* the meanings in experience; he has learned to *make* meanings:

> . . . I had a conception of life that no experience would ever erase, a predilection for what was real that no argument could

> ever gainsay, a sense of the world that was mine and mine
> alone, a notion as to what life meant that no education could
> ever alter, a conviction that the meaning of living came only
> when one was struggling to wring a meaning out of
> meaningless suffering. (112)

He may have begun to learn this lesson at the age of twelve, as he said,
but, like most important lessons, he took many years to understand
fully the implications of being an artist, one who rejects the option of
responding impulsively for the challenge of struggling reflectively.

At the end of *Black Boy*, then, we are left with a simple, youthful
gesture, described in simple, youthful words of excess. But this very
simplicity reveals the book's Longinian tendencies. For we have been
taken on a circuitous journey, beginning with childhood, "the long-ago
four-year-old days" of Richard Wright's life, propelled to adulthood, to
"that day a quarter of a century later," and left with adolescence,
Wright's "running more away from something than toward something."
Perhaps this finale was only a hasty addition, but perhaps there is
another way to evaluate the conclusion that is really no conclusion.
Might it be a sign of the artist, Richard Wright, communing with his
many selves, past and present, and , at the same time, being affected by
the various voices that characterized these past and present selves? If
the voice we hear at the end is indeed a new voice, if it is mystical and
youthful and excessive and optimistic, perhaps it is also distorted,
distorted by the sights and sounds of a cavernous hall of mirrors in
which the autobiographer lives as he tries to make meaning of the
multiple selves called Richard Wright.

AMERICAN HUNGER

Wright's second autobiography, originally called *The Horror and
the Glory*, emphasizes the labyrinthine journey of self-creation even
more than *Black Boy*. In the snarling labyrinth is the hero, a virtual
fairy-tale hero, who finds himself in a fantasy world, "an unreal city
whose mythical houses were built of slabs of black coal wreathed in
palls of gray smoke, houses whose foundations were sinking slowly
into the dank prairie."[13]   This opening vision of a nightmarish
dreamscape echoes throughout the book. At the end of the first chapter,
the narrator recalls his self-knowledge, which prevented him from

having "easily lost my way in the fogbound regions of compelling fantasy," and in subsequent chapters he remembers how others were "wandering in a fantasy," were "black and lost," were "lost in a fantasy." The narrator is thus reconstructing a journey that is similar to the archetypical search of a hero with a thousand faces: Richard Wright sets out, possessed of some self-knowledge and aware of the importance of his quest, to achieve his goal.

The search is not easy, however; even with his self-knowledge, he has setbacks: "I floundered, staggered," but the hero continues: "somehow I always groped my way back to that path where I felt a tinge of warmth from an unseen light." If we were left with this movement from darkness to light, we would have an Aristotelian autobiography, a recreation of the heroic journey in classical terms. But that is not the case. At the end of *American Hunger*, we are left with the darkness and silence of night and the empty page, the ultimate tribute to the unfinished quality of a self in process:

> I sat alone in my narrow room, watching the sun sink slowly in the chilly May sky. . . .
> I picked up a pencil and held it over a sheet of white paper, but my feelings stood in the way of my words. Well, I would wait, day and night, until I knew what to say. Humbly now, with no vaulting dream of achieving a vast unity, I wanted to try to build a bridge of words between me and the world outside, that world which was so distant and elusive that it seemed unreal. I would hurl words into this darkness and wait for an echo, and if an echo sounded, no matter how faintly, I would send other words to tell, to march, to fight, to create a sense of the hunger for life that gnaws in us all, to keep alive in our hearts a sense of the inexpressibly human. (134–5)

"With no vaulting dream of achieving a vast unity": this phrase captures the essence of Wright's autobiographical style and his autobiographical hero. In a world of continual efforts to reduce complexities, connect discrete parts, reduce everything and everyone to a simple, unified whole, Wright the author and Wright the character choose the labyrinth of complexity over the straight road of simplicity. They choose the darkness of ambiguity over the lightness of clarity.

The choice of complexity is really many choices, including linguistic, psychological, political, social. Wright learns that wrestling with language, "the single aim of my living," was similar to wrestling with other significant realities: every struggle was an effort to destroy simplistic polarities. And every polarity, in Wright's view, is related to the ultimate American duality, the Negro paradox.

> Though he is an organic part of the nation, he is excluded by the entire tide and direction of American culture. Frankly, it is felt to be right to exclude him, and it is felt to be wrong to admit him freely. Therefore, if within the confines of its present culture, the nation ever seeks to purge itself of its color hate, it will find itself at war with itself, convulsed by a spasm of emotional and moral confusion. If the nation ever finds itself examining its real relation to the Negro, it will find itself doing infinitely more than that; for the anti-Negro attitude of whites represents but a tiny part—though a symbolically significant one—of the moral attitude of the nation. Our too-young and too-new America, lusty because it is lonely, aggressive because it is afraid, insists upon seeing the world in terms of good and bad, the holy and the evil, the high and the low, the white and the black; our America is frightened of fact, of history, of processes, of necessity. (13–14)

Fearing complexity, then, Wright's enemies hide behind shields of linguistic, political, psychological, and social polarities, challenging Richard Wright the young warrior to attack their phalanxes. He must learn which weapons to use. For the artist as a young man, the decision becomes clear: he will use language "to tell, to march, to fight."

And there is much to fight against. There is "the general Communist analysis of the world," which Wright cannot refute in toto but which he sees as "just too simple for belief." Reducing past and future into one simplistic today, the Communists' "only task was to annihilate the enemy that confronted them in any manner possible." When the abstract enemy becomes the concrete individual, when it becomes Wright and people he respects, the warrior decides to look for a different militia to join.

Another enemy to fight against is the dominant culture, the American authoritative culture which demonstrates its simplistic view of superiority in multitudinous ways, including its lineup of people in institutions like the hospital in which Wright worked.

A line of white girls marched past, clad in starched uniforms that gleamed white; their faces were alert, their steps quick, their bodies lean and shapely, their shoulders erect, their faces lit with the light of purpose. And after them came a line of black girls, old, fat, dressed in ragged gingham, walking loosely, carrying tin cans of soap powder, rags, mops, brooms . . . I wondered what law of the universe kept them from being mixed? (46)

But if this "law of the universe," promulgated by white simplistic fear, was an enemy, so, too, was the Negro attitude that Wright confronted when, for instance, he talked with a co-worker at the hospital about the race problem. The black man's solution? "'Let the government give every man a gun and five bullets, then let us all start over again. Make it just like it was in the beginning. The ones who come out on top, white or black, let them rule'" (47). Wright can only respond to this attitude by acknowledging his terror at its simplicity.

The third chapter of *American Hunger* is an important key to understanding Wright's fear of reductionistic philosophies. Like the first chapter of *Black Boy*, this chronicle of Wright's job as an orderly to a medical research institute in a large, wealthy hospital in Chicago is a neat synecdoche. Its images of black and white girls lined up in polarized structures and its dialogue between the searching Wright and the dogmatic co-worker who advocates guns and bullets as the means for survival highlight the irrationality of a simplistic universe.

This universe is dangerous not just because of its deceptive neatness but because of its consequences for humanity. As Wright points out in this important chapter, avoiding complexity means avoiding individuality. Thus Wright, as orderly, is commanded to work efficiently and mindlessly while a boy stands over him, timing his movements with a stop watch. The boy and the director who had ordered the surveillance did not, in Wright's words, regard him as a human being but rather as a machine to be timed by another machine. Silently dehumanized, Wright is no different from the dogs who were devocalized so that their howls would not disturb the patients in the hospital. Their soundless wail, Wright wrote, "became lodged in my imagination as a symbol of silent suffering" (48). Questioning this procedure of devocalizing the dogs, the young orderly was ignored. His questions, his being, his identity—all were ignored.

A curious quality of this simplistic view of life, this belief in neatness and control at all costs, is its ignorance of the chaos and lack of control that Wright sees as inherent in the human condition. While bureaucrats are avoiding intelligent questions, using stop watches to evaluate productivity, and lining people up on the basis of the color of their skin, they are unaware of an unpredictability that is beneath their scientifically controlled experiments. The last part of Chapter 3 is a marvelously humorous and insightful example of the facade of control being undermined by fundamental chaos. Wright and his co-workers are in the room with the cages of devocalized dogs when the two elderly co-workers who had been in a state of constant, irrational, unfocused quarreling begin an outright fight. In the midst of the fight, the animal-filled steel tier is toppled and the doors of the cages swing open, releasing most of the animals and killing others that were hurled beneath the tier. To keep their jobs, the workers have to dispose of the dead animals and somehow sort the rats and mice that were cancerous, the dogs that were diabetic, the Ascheim-Zondeck rabbits, and the Wasserman guinea pigs. While they know that certain rats or mice go into certain cages, they do not know *which* rats or mice go into *what* cage. The white doctors had made sure that they would not know: "They had never taken time to answer a single question; though we worked in the institute, we were as remote from the meaning of the experiments as if we lived in the moon. The doctors had laughed at what they felt was our childlike interest in the fate of the animals" (56).

If they do not know the cages into which they should put the animals, they know that they have to take some action, and, in the basement of a great scientific institution, they hold a remarkable meeting: "It was a strange scientific conference; the fate of the entire medical research institute rested in our ignorant, black hands." Methodically putting animals in cages that *look* like the right cages, the workers put the room back in order and wait for hours and then days for their secret to be discovered. But in this orderly, controlled, systematic, scientific world, nothing is spotted. The only questions are asked by the autobiographer:

> Was some scientific hypothesis, well on its way to validation and ultimate public use, discarded because of unexpected findings on that cold winter day? Was some tested principle given a new and strange refinement because of fresh, remarkable evidence? Did some brooding research worker—those who held stop

watches and slopped their feet carelessly in the water of the
steps I tried too hard to keep clean—get a wild, if brief,
glimpse of a new scientific truth? Well, we never heard. . . .
(58)

The hospital's silence not only continues to conceal the inherent
unpredictability of behavior, but it also forces the orderlies to create—to
create their "own code of ethics, values, loyalty." The ongoing battle
continues, a war between the satisfied and the hungry, between control
and creation.

In this complicated warfare, Wright learns that he must be a
solitary fighter, a lonely writer. "Writing had to be done in loneliness,"
he acknowledges, "and Communism had declared war upon human
loneliness. Alone, they said, a man was weak; united with others, he
was strong. Therefore they habitually feared a man who stood alone"
(123). Standing alone, "really alone now," as he says at the end of
American Hunger, Richard Wright knows that he cannot align himself
with any one party, race, or ideology. "I had outgrown my childhood,"
he writes, suggesting that he had also outgrown his need for political,
racial, and other identities. The autobiographical hero has learned to
think of himself not as a Negro but as a writer, not as a social being
but as a solitary craftsman, not as a member of a party but as a
spokesman for the human heart who would survive because he would
write: "Perhaps, I thought, out of my tortured feelings I could fling a
spark into this darkness. I would try, not because I wanted to but
because I felt that I had to if I were to live at all" (134).

His writing would be a special kind now that he has seen the need
for his solitary transcendence. Remembering the stories he had written,
the stories in which he had given honor and glory to the Communist
party, he rejoices that they were "finished." For he can no longer write
such neat, predictable products again: "I knew in my heart that I would
never be able to write that way again, would never be able to feel with
that simple sharpness about life, would never again express such
passionate hope, would never again make so total a commitment of
faith" (133). Instead, his approach and theme will be process, the
unfinished quality of the self in search of itself.

Black Hunger, the nonbook that includes both autobiographical
volumes, ends with darkness, a blank sheet of paper, and ambiguous
words like "distant" and "elusive" and "unreal." It also ends with
"hunger," the recognition that the self is not filled, satisfied, contented.

The emptiness that is the writer's commitment "to create a sense of the hunger for life that gnaws in us all" is also the writer's admission that darkness, blankness, and emptiness are both the end and the beginning of the autobiographical journey. "They meet with darkness in the daytime/And they grope at noonday as in the night," the epigraph to *Black Hunger*, reflects the circularity of William Carlos Williams' description of memory as well as Richard Wright's two-part "Record of Childhood and Youth." The descent does beckon, on that "winter morning in the long-ago" and the ascent does beckon, on that evening in chilly May. Richard Wright is meeting Richard Wright "with darkness in the daytime" and they, the multiple selves of yesterday and today, are groping "at noonday as in the night."

Notes

1. James Olney, "The Ontology of Autobiography," in *Autobiography: Essays Theoretical and Critical* (Princeton: Princeton University Press, 1980), 248.
2. In her book *The Art of Life: Studies in American Autobiographical Literature* (Austin & London: University of Texas Press, 1977), Mutlu Konuk Blasing quotes this passage from *Paterson* to reinforce her assertion that autobiographers do not simply repeat the past when they write about it; they also create it, for, as she puts it, "memory looks out upon new landscapes" (159).
3. Richard Wright to Paul Reynolds, December 17, 1943, quoted in the Afterword to *American Hunger* by Michel Fabre (New York: Harper and Row, 1977), 143.
4. Michel Fabre's indispensable biography, *The Unfinished Quest of Richard Wright* (New York: William Morrow & Company, 1973), relates the process by which the two books were published separately, including the dilemma about titles. According to Fabre, Aswell wanted to add an explanatory subtitle, "The Biography of a Courageous Negro," to the title *Black Boy*, but Wright objected, saying that he wanted the reader to be the judge of his courage. He first suggested the alternative subtitle of "Biography of an American Negro," and then later proposed other possibilities: "Coming of Age in the Black South," "Coming of Age in the

Black Belt," "Growing up in the Black South," "The Story of a Southern Childhood," "A Record in Anxiety," "A Study in Anxiety," "Odyssey of a Southern Childhood," and "A Chronicle of Anxiety" (Fabre 254–255).

5. Richard Wright, "The Birth of *Black Boy*," *New York Post*, November 30, 1944, quoted in Afterword to *American Hunger*, 138.
6. Michel Fabre, Afterword to *American Hunger* by Richard Wright (New York: Harper and Row, 1977), 138.
7. Northrop Frye discusses these two views of literature in an essay entitled "Towards Defining an Age of Sensibility," in *Fables of Identity: Studies in Poetic Mythology* (New York: Harcourt, Brace and World, 1963).
8. Elizabeth Schultz, "To Be Black and Blue: The Blues Genre in Black Autobiography" in *Kansas Quarterly*, 7, no. 3 (Summer 1975): 81–96. Reprinted in *The American Autobiography:A Collection of Critical Essays*, edited by Albert E. Stone (Englewood Cliffs: Prentice-Hall, 1981), 109–132.
9. Sidonie Ann Smith, "Richard Wright's *Black Boy*: The Creative Impulse as Rebellion" in *The Southern Literary Journal* (1972): 123–136; and Roger Rosenblatt, "Black Autobiography: Life as the Death Weapon" in *The Yale Review* 65 (1976): 515–527.
10. Albert Stone, *Autobiographical Occasions and Original Acts: Versions of American Identity from Henry Adams to Nate Shaw* (Philadelphia: University of Pennsylvania Press, 1982), 124.
11. Richard Wright, *Black Boy* (New York: Harper and Row, 1945), 12. Subsequent references are inserted parenthetically.
12. Horace A. Porter demonstrates how *Black Boy* is a *kunstle roman* in his essay "The Horror and the Glory: Richard Wright's Portrait of the Artist in *Black Boy* and *American Hunger*." He argues that the theme of words is the main motif of the book, the nucleus around which ancillary themes move. See "The Horror and the Glory" in *Richard Wright: A Collection of Critical Essays*, edited by Richard Macksey and Frank E. Moorer (Englewood Cliffs: Prentice-Hall, Inc., 1984), 55–67.

13. Richard Wright, *American Hunger* (New York: Harper and Row, 1977), 1. Afterword by Michel Fabre. Subsequent references are inserted parenthetically.

Articulation and Collaboration in Richard Wright's Major Fiction

Alison Rieke

Questions about Richard Wright's tendency toward polemics, both in the "Fate" section of *Native Son* and in various parts of *The Outsider*, appear in criticism with predictable frequency, even though Wright insisted that black American writing should be political. Wright's lack of subtlety disturbs some critics who have accused him of being unable to sustain a detached artistic voice, of needing to tell us what his books mean.[1] Wright closes *Native Son* with strong political statements: Max's views produce an abstract version of the "meaning" of the first two sections of the novel, and his speech stimulates critical commentary precisely because Wright ceases to show and begins to tell what Bigger's life means.[2] In *The Outsider*, Wright also tells us what Cross Damon represents, a more blatant treatment than in *Native Son*. Do these passages show lapses in artistic judgment and are they fictionally inappropriate? Political statements and counterstatements are not entirely out of place in works that directly engage political concerns. But can context give these passages validity, despite the fact that this level of argumentation strikes many readers as intrusive? Wright did sustain a fictional demonstration of his politics in the first two sections of *Native Son* and in the brilliant novella, *The Man Who Lived Underground*, where political positions are acted out rather than argued verbally. From these two works it does seem that Wright was capable of making clear choices about how to present his material. Here I will address the question of Wright's polemics, which may have a clear place within a narrative structure repeated in three major texts: *Native Son, The Outsider*, and *The Man Who Lived Underground*. This narrative pattern sheds some light upon Wright's problematic shifts from showing to telling.

A narrative shift from showing to telling occurs when Wright's protagonists feel compelled to confess their crimes. In terms of narrative design, they tell in order to elicit a collaborative response from the person or people receiving privileged confessions. Quite consciously, Wright gives his protagonists mouthpieces who are, in turn, delegated the role of communicating what has been told to them. For Wright's protagonists, these moments of articulation are necessary, and they serve to link isolated men to the outside world. In *Native Son* and *The Outsider*, the collaborators are prepared to make statements to the world. At the close of *Native Son*, Bigger's collaborator, Boris Max, asks him, "Is there anything you want me to do on the outside? Any message you want to send?" (385).[3] And when Cross Damon lies on his deathbed in *The Outsider*, Houston asks him, "Is there anything, Damon, you want me to tell anybody?" (439).[4] However, Wright's narratives begin to spill outside their fictional frames at precisely this moment of telling, and, in this case, "outside" begins to mean "the outside world" or "those who need to be told outside this novel." Thus, telling undermines the fictional construct and serves a double purpose: that of offering commentary to people both inside and outside the texts.

As Wright's narrative plan progresses up to articulation and collaboration, his protagonists move through a series of steps that can be outlined in the following way: (1) Fear leads to an act of violence or a crime, and this act liberates or recreates the self. (2) This act results in a period of concealment in which the protagonists explore their feelings about the crime. (3) The need to conceal immediately gives way to the desire to tell, to articulate the act, and thereby find its meaning and justification. (4) Articulation, however, engenders the need for a collaborator whose understanding of the crime will prove to the protagonists that they are not alone. (5) Collaboration points toward the possibility of the protagonists' reintegration into a rejecting society. In these works, however, reintegration does not occur in a satisfying or complete way; it remains, at best, a hope, a projection into the future. If and when the protagonists do achieve human contact, their terrible sense of exclusion will diminish and eventually disappear. However, the world of the novel and the world at large are inextricably bound together, even if confused with each other, in Wright's fictional moments of articulation and collaboration. When Wright's polemics disrupt the fictional frame, his narratives suggest that no change can occur inside his fictions until some corresponding action is taken outside their boundaries. Wright's violation of the fictional frame, intentional or not, demonstrates the inadequacy of art to change life.

The first two stages of this narrative plan have been especially important in commentaries on Bigger Thomas's dilemma in *Native Son*, which turns upon the notion that fear leads to an act of violence. As Mr. Max tells the judge in his courtroom speech, fear engenders Bigger's crimes: "Fear and hate and guilt are the keynotes of this drama" (357). In *The Outsider,* Cross Damon describes this same fear: "He [man] is the most scared and trembling of all the animals. . . . It might well be that the most important part of human existence is fear itself . . ." (356–57). Damon's words describe the state of anxiety overwhelming Bigger Thomas at crucial points leading up to his crime. This fear engulfs Bigger in the courtroom when he is faced with a sea of white men: ". . . constricted, taut, in the grip of a powerful, impelling fear. . . . He wanted to leap from his chair and swing some heavy weapon and end this unequal fight" (344).

The second step in Wright's narrative plan, concealment and self-discovery, has also received substantial coverage and perhaps has been given too much emphasis in analyses of *Native Son.*[5] Bigger's determined and calculated evasion of detection, his flight, and his reflections upon his act (which are represented through objective narration) all express this state. Bigger's self-discoveries are summarized in Boris Max's statement about the crime: "But, after he murdered, he accepted the crime. And that's the important thing. It was the first full act of his life: it was the most meaningful, exciting and stirring thing that had ever happened to him" (364); "It was an act of *creation*!" (366). Bigger's story, however, does not culminate in self-discovery. His impulse toward articulation and collaboration takes him a step beyond an existential moment of awareness, but these concerns have received limited attention in criticism, and the assumption that "the big question of Book III is whether Bigger will find himself" dominates the scholarship of *Native Son.*[6] Donald B. Gibson, for instance, claims that "the focus of the novel is not on the trial nor on Max, but on Bigger and on his finally successful attempt to come to terms with his imminent death."[7] Yet after Wright explores the need for self-discovery and self-mastery, he advances to the results of articulating that discovery. Can Bigger adequately articulate the meaning of his crime? Will anyone understand him and then collaborate with him against the tremendous pressures of a hostile world? Will an enemy in his own country benefit from telling about his crime? And finally, will the exclusion of the Bigger Thomases continue?

Articulation is such an enormous problem for Bigger that Wright chooses several spokesmen for him. In fact, this problem works its way into Wright's handling of narrators. Bigger's inarticulate voice contrasts with the third-person narrator's: ". . . the narrator, at the most crucial points of action and self-recognition, becomes a sort of translator, or refiner, perhaps, of the stifled, muddled intensity of Bigger's inner life."[8] Max's voice, "the highly articulate and humane voice . . . supremely analytical," must also be separated from Bigger's.[9] Bigger himself, at the time of his impending death, is only beginning to realize he has a voice; hence, his language is halting, frustrated, and reluctant. Clearly Bigger is not entirely ready to speak for himself, so Wright gives him Max. But Max is also pushing his own concerns, and finally we must isolate those moments when he actually speaks for Bigger, not for himself or the party.

Yet Bigger does try to speak, for an unfulfilled desire to communicate lies behind his frustration and hopelessness. But because Bigger cannot yet articulate for himself and because Max does not fully understand him, Wright appropriately develops these passages through third-person omniscient narration. Wright obviously wants Bigger to be understood by someone, and the information the narrator provides increases the chance that Bigger's message will be heard. Wright uses a fictional voice that articulates even when those within the fictional frame cannot: "His lips trembled to speak, to tell Max to leave; but no words came. He felt that even in speaking in that way he would be indicating how hopeless he felt, thereby disrobing his soul to more shame" (320). Bigger's need to speak, the impulse to reveal the interior self, is much stronger than the constraints of inarticulate speech: "His talking to Max had evoked again in him that urge to talk, to tell, to try to make his feelings known. A wave of excitement flooded him. He felt that he ought to be able to reach out . . ." (323). For Bigger, this act of articulation is an entirely new, but indissoluble part of his need to express *why* he killed: ". . . it was not until after Max had gone that he discovered that he had spoken to Max as he had never spoken to anyone in his life; not even himself. And his talking had eased from his shoulders a heavy burden" (333). Nevertheless, Bigger's feelings are so mixed toward the unfamiliar act of speech that he immediately recoils with mistrust: "Then he was suddenly violently angry. Max had tricked him! But no. Max had not compelled him to talk; he had talked of his own accord . . ." (333). Bigger has spoken by choice and realizes it, and this act opens up the new possibility that he will be heard.

Talk alone can link Bigger with the culture that has excluded him. Max appeals to the court's duty to hear Bigger: "Shall we deny this boy, because he is poor and black, the same protection, the same chance to be heard and understood that we have so readily granted to others?" (348). Throughout the "Fate" section of *Native Son*, Wright's insistence that his readers listen to Bigger echoes in the words "talk," "tell," "hear," and "speak." But ironically, Wright purposefully excludes Max's speech from Bigger's own understanding, and in doing so, Wright stresses Bigger's immature self awareness: "He had not understood the speech, but he had felt the meaning of some of it from the tone of Max's voice" (370). For Bigger, and no doubt for Wright, its significance lies not in the content of the words but in the act itself, the fact that talking about the Bigger Thomases in America is an action worth more than the words: "He was hugging the proud thought that Max had made the speech all for him, to save his life. It was not the meaning of the speech that gave him pride, but the mere act of it" (371).

The final scenes of *Native Son* reinforce Bigger's increasing need to articulate, a need which Wright reiterates at each significant point in Bigger's contact with Max. The knowledge of his approaching death again sets into motion the desire for talk. First reluctant, Bigger "could not talk about this thing, so elusive it was . . ." (384); but then, "why didn't he speak now? Here was his chance, his last chance" (385); and again, "He stood up, full now, wanting to talk. His lips moved, but no words came" (385). When he finally does speak, "he tried to charge into the tone of his words what he *himself* wanted to hear, what *he* needed" (388).

A step beyond articulation is understanding and even empathy. Bigger is unprepared for Max's failure to respond to him: "Max did not even *know*!"(387). After his protagonists have spoken, Wright hopes that they will elicit a just response from the world, not only agreement but also collaboration. The word *collaborate* is perfectly applicable to the relationship between Wright's protagonists and the people they tell:

it means "to work together," especially in a joint intellectual effort, and to cooperate treasonably, as with an enemy occupying one's own country. Wright uses "collaboration" in *The Man Who Lived Underground* in precisely these terms, and he implies it in Bigger Thomas' and Cross Damon's quests for complete understanding. They seek men who will comprehend the complex emotions behind their crimes. Certainly, Wright views the black man's position in America as one of an enemy in his own country. The "Fate" section of *Native Son* records the attempted collaboration of Max and Bigger, which remains only partial. It cannot be fulfilled, Wright says, because Max does not completely accept Bigger. Wright, willing at this point to admit the possibility of full understanding, explores a relationship that cannot meet that goal.

Max succeeds in collaborating with Bigger in that he willingly speaks for the black man in America. As Bigger is the enemy, so also will Max become the enemy of the majority culture when he publicly sympathizes with Bigger. But Max's speech only generalizes Bigger's act into a larger political significance, and it is here that Max's understanding falls short of Wright's idea of a completed moment of collaboration. Max's collaboration fails when he attempts to understand the deeper emotional content of Bigger's crime. Bigger's brief statement of his feelings at the close of the novel baffles Max, leaving him bewildered and scared: "Bigger saw Max back away from him with compressed lips" (391). Max's collaboration must falter, and indeed his "eyes were full of terror" (392) when Bigger asserts that his crime is integral to his identity.

Fred Daniels, the protagonist of Wright's *The Man Who Lived Underground*, experiences a similar version of this movement from fear and "terrible exclusion," through crime and concealment, to self-discovery. He, too, finds excitement and meaning in the idea of telling and of collaborating his crime. But his collaborator is a delusion and the vision destroys him. For Fred Daniels, collaboration is a form of projection, wherein he thrusts his desire for understanding onto an object rather than a person. Daniels' urge to reveal his secret duplicates Bigger's desire to tell. But in *The Man Who Lived Underground*, this narrative moment takes a bitter turn, for objects are only objects, and Daniels' discoveries about his crime touch no one who can help him.

The false collaboration of the jewels Daniels has stolen occurs in his underground world, where he imagines that they condone his theft as he infuses life and feeling into them. But this ironic collaboration mocks any real understanding: "The blue and white sparks from the stones filled the cave with brittle laughter, as though enjoying his hilarious secret" (550), and "He stooped and flung the diamonds more evenly over the floor and they showered rich sparks, collaborating with him" (551).[10] The collaboration of the stones seems a "glorious victory," and it allows Daniels to consider that "maybe anything's right. . . . Yes, if the world as men had made it was right, then anything else was right, any act a man took to satisfy himself, murder, theft, torture" (551). Daniels' delusion undermines him completely when he returns to the above-ground world and expects other men to listen to him and to understand.

Daniels' later impulse to tell about his experiences almost seems a bitter comment upon Bigger Thomas' attempts to communicate. Daniels has no lawyer to tell, but he decides he must tell someone and so chooses his accusers, the police. The inevitable desire to speak overcomes Daniels in the isolating, inhuman underground: "He shuddered, feeling that, in spite of his fear, sooner or later he would go up into that dead sunshine and somehow say something to somebody about all this" (553); and "sleeping within him was the drive to go somewhere and say something to somebody" (560–561).

Once in a position to tell about his experience in the underground, Daniels finds that no one can understand him. His mutterings are inarticulate, unable to express the deeply complex series of visions and discoveries that came to him in the underground: "He spoke like a child relating a dimly remembered dream" (563). Daniels' inability to speak reinforces his isolation: "But how could he say it? The distance between what he felt and what these men meant was vast . . . he would never be able to tell them . . . they would never believe him even if he told them" (565). This horrible lack of contact causes Daniels to panic. Telling is not enough; when he speaks to the police, he needs a deeper understanding: "He saw that they were not understanding what he was saying. He grew frantic to make them believe . . ." (568). He feels he can remedy the problem of inarticulation by showing the men the underground: "They would see what he had seen; they would feel what he had felt" (573). This desire for a collaborator costs Daniels a fatal mistake: these men will not listen, and Daniels was correct at the moment he realized the "images" in the cave would not "have the meaning for others that they had for him" (572). The police shoot him

and send him to an obscure, meaningless death down into the swirl of
sewer water in the underground.

The *Outsider* offers a more complex arrangement of Wright's
narrative progression, primarily because Cross Damon's crimes are less
motivated by fear than by its opposite, the power of the "little god."
Also, Damon is more articulate than either Bigger Thomas or Fred
Daniels; he does speak for himself, commanding the respect and fear of
the people he meets. Scenes involving confession and silence,
Damon's alternating need to give information and to withhold crucial
revelations about himself, occur with particular frequency in this novel,
especially toward its close. The final section of *The Outsider*,
"Decision," is structured primarily around scenes of disclosure and
withholding, such as the long interrogation of Cross Damon (378-94).
And Wright links the act of confession with the most violent impulses
in his protagonist: "There were to be no more of those torrid
promptings of his heart to make him confess his horrible deeds and then
wrestle and sweat to restrain his urge to kill the recipient of his
confession" (375). Fundamentally, Wright takes Damon through the
same series of steps as his other two protagonists.[11] Wright presents
his hero's moment of articulation in a long ideological speech which
becomes a public comment to the Communists. And Wright gives
Damon a real collaborator, who can simultaneously speak for and break
through the isolation of the Wright protagonist.

But Wright first explores Damon's need to tell someone about his
crimes through the character of Eva Blount. Damon's choice of Eva as
his confessor is born of her love and trust for him. It is her insistence
upon trust, however, that finally disqualifies her as a true collaborator.
She, like Boris Max, is unable to accept the personal confession of a
murderer. But Damon persistently asks that she hear him: "He yearned
for the sight of Eva. If only he could talk to somebody! To wander
always alone was too much. . . . He knew he had to tell her everything
now: he *had* to tell . . ." (317). He returns to Eva's apartment with the
confession on his lips: "He knew that he wanted to spill it all out,
everything. . . . Oh, God, such trust in that face . . . How could he tell
her?" (319). And the words work their way out of him—"'I *must* talk,'
he said, 'I must tell you—Darling, I killed your husband . . .'" (320)—
but Eva does not believe him.

In *The Outsider* Wright duplicates the narrative moment of
confession several times, but again in an important scene involving

Eva. Damon is possessed by his need for Eva's understanding, but ironically he destroys her with his final and complete articulation of his crimes; this occurs immediately after he has refused to speak openly to District Attorney Houston (394). With Houston, Damon restrains himself from the temptation to tell in order to survive: but this pent-up desire sends him back to Eva. He comes to her directly from the D. A.'s office: "Could he ever tell her? He had to try. He had to talk or he could not go on living" (398). Damon, determined to say it all to Eva, knows she has wanted to provide him with a link to humanity, but by the time he is ready to tell everything, she is not able to hear or understand the horrifying details of his confession.

Once again Wright's protagonist needs to be understood completely. But the pressure upon Eva to acknowledge and collaborate with the acts themselves sends her through a window to her death. Damon asks her to empathize: "'Eva, I'm praying to you to try to understand me. . . . Oh, Christ. I can't explain it! You have to *feel* it! You have to *live* it!'" (399). Whether or not both Sara and Eva had collaborated with Damon's crimes when they too wished Gil and Hilton dead (289-91) means nothing in Wright's final assessment of understanding. Eva simply cannot accept the idea of murder, and she remains outside the outsider. With her and in her Damon has no collaborator against the laws that would judge him guilty.

Wright creates another version of Bigger Thomas' collaborator, Boris Max, in District Attorney Houston. This man, because of physical deformity, feels kinship with the black man in America, particularly the criminal black man. Wright wishes to find the person who can fulfill the role of collaborator, and in Houston he seems to have succeeded. Wright accomplishes this full collaboration by making his D. A. identify with Damon and then articulate the exact circumstances and motivations of Damon's killings. Once again, the legal arena provides the backdrop for speaking, but ironically, Houston speaks for Damon by not speaking: he decides not to expose Damon's crimes. In scene after scene, Damon's feelings toward Houston are charged with conflicting fear and excitement because Damon knows this man can reveal his crimes. Despite the fact that Houston says he has no concrete proof against Damon to use in a court of law (429-430), Wright's decision to let Houston hide Damon's crimes from "due process of law" confirms collaboration, for Houston is truly in league with the criminal when he determines that the isolated man should pass judgment upon himself: "It's between *you* and *you*, you and yourself" (430). Houston admits that he was Damon's "unwitting accomplice for seventy-two hours" (418), as he proceeds to articulate Damon's activities and crimes with complete accuracy. Moments of identification occur in Houston's telling: "But the more I pondered this thing, the sorrier I felt for you. I began to feel as though I'd killed Blount, Herndon, and Hilton myself" (421).

Ironically, when Houston lets Damon off the legal hook, Damon becomes frantic at the thought of his aloneness. He fears that the world will not know of his crimes, and thus collaboration will dissolve back into isolation. Wright uses the word *collaborate* in a new context in *The Outsider* to show the tragic circularity of aloneness, the black man's return to self from the fleeting community of only one other collaborator: "Suddenly he wanted to beg this man not to leave him" (430), and "He had to talk to somebody! But to whom? No; he had to keep this crime choked in his throat. He, like others, had to pretend that nothing like this could ever happen; he had to collaborate and help keep the secret" (431). Damon asks, ". . . was it possible that all he had learned in the last few weeks would remain locked forever in his heart? Would he ever be able to say anything about it?" (434). When Damon lies on his deathbed, the victim of Communist assassins, Houston appears at his side to hear the final message Damon leaves with the world. In Houston, Wright creates a collaborator who does not look on with terror and then retreat into silence. Houston asks Damon, echoing Max in *Native Son*, "Is there anything, Damon, you want me to tell anybody?" (439). Damon answers at least with the full knowledge that Houston understands him. Nevertheless, Wright heavily qualifies the position of the protagonist, even one with a genuine collaborator.

Criticism of *Native Son* and *The Outsider* stresses the theme of the "outsider," the existential problem of self in relation to community. Whether the outsider be a black man may not matter to Wright, considering his portrayal of Houston, but the black protagonist is especially prone to a "deep sense of exclusion"[12] that must be counteracted if he is to find his place in America. The remedy to exclusion begins in this narrative pattern with one collaborator, by necessity a white man (not a white woman: Wright explores that possibility and rejects it in the portrait of Eva Blount) because only he can provide the link with a rejecting majority culture. This is all

Bigger Thomas, Fred Daniels, and Cross Damon ask for in their struggles to free themselves from the exclusion, guilt, and fear America has bequeathed them.

Wright's treatment of collaboration in *The Man Who Lived Underground* is deeply pessimistic in that Daniels seems doomed to be misunderstood from the outset: the men Daniels tries to tell represent the essence of the vast system in America which has excluded and condemned men like him. *Native Son* ends more optimistically by offering Bigger Thomas a spokesman who does convey something of the plight of the American black, even if he cannot communicate fully Bigger's personal dilemma. The "Fate" section of *Native Son* tells us that someone must step forward to make public speeches for the Bigger Thomases in America and that partial understanding is better than none at all. The Bigger Thomases need to tell about themselves, but they also need others to tell for them because they "had lived outside of the lives of men. Their modes of communication, their symbols and images, had been denied" them (386). Yet collaboration must finally be shown, acted out, not just told: in political terms, Wright's fiction progresses up to words about understanding and collaboration, not to actions that confirm the black man's place in a community of Americans. In fact, all three works assert the black man's existential aloneness. Houston, too, is an outsider, and he is only one man. His collaboration with Damon isolates him from his community and from the legal system that should govern both of them.

Wright viewed his role as a writer in precisely the terms of the collaborator. He found his commitment to art in a parallel commitment to tell about and to collaborate the crimes of Bigger: "I would hurl words into this darkness and wait for an echo; and if an echo sounded, no matter how faintly, I would send other words to tell, to march, to fight, to create a sense of the hunger for life that gnaws in us all, to keep alive in our hearts a sense of the inexpressibly human."[13] Wright may have tried to become a Communist because he saw in its politics a partial collaboration with the black man in America. Communism failed Wright because the methods it used to act out ideas conflicted with the very ideas it articulated, but he used his anti-Communist novel, *The Outsider*, to continue the quest for a collaborator and for reintegration. Wright's narrative pattern holds out the hope of counteracting exclusion and despair, a hope that is verbalized but not fully realized as action. When District Attorney

Houston asks Cross Damon if there is anything to tell, Damon answers: "Tell them not to come down this road. . . . Man is all we've got. . . . I'm legion. . . . I've lived alone, but I'm everywhere . . ." (439-40). Damon can depend upon the fact that Houston will neither slant nor misconstrue the meaning of this horrible, "deep sense of exclusion." Finally, it is human contact that these men find so necessary. Through Bigger Thomas and Cross Damon and Fred Daniels, Richard Wright speaks not for rebellion and existential criminality, which traps all three protagonists in prisons of isolation, but for reintegration of the excluded American. They feel loss and emptiness where there should be human communication and compassion. As Wright expressed it in *American Hunger*, "I headed toward home alone, really alone now, telling myself that in all the sprawling immensity of our mighty continent the least-known factor of living was the human heart, the least-sought goal of being was a way to live a human life. Perhaps, I thought, out of my tortured feelings I could fling a spark into this darkness."[14]

Notes

1. Katherine Fishburn in *Richard Wright's Hero: The Faces of a Rebel-Victim* (Metuchen, N.J.: Scarecrow Press, 1977), expresses a typically condescending view of Wright's "Fate" section: "When Wright begins his narrative of Bigger's trial he slips into the pitfall of preaching to the reader—a flaw seen in much proletarian writing. Up until this point in the book Wright had allowed Bigger and the facts of his existence to speak for themselves. But here Wright apparently felt he could not rely on his reader's perceptive abilities, so he steps in to *tell* him what the book has been about" (69).

2. Paul N. Siegel in "The Conclusion of Richard Wright's *Native Son*," *PMLA*, 89 (1974), 517-523, corrects the critical assumption that Max gives the "party line." Other helpful treatments of the "Fate" section of *Native Son* are Edward Kearns' "The Fate Section of *Native Son*," *Contemporary Literature*, 12 (Spring 1971), 146-155; and Donald B. Gibson's "Wright's Invisible *Native Son*," *American Quarterly*, 21 (Winter 1969), 728-738. The articles by Siegel and Gibson are reprinted in

Richard Wright: A Collection of Critical Essays, ed. Richard Macksey and Frank E. Moorer (Englewood Cliffs, N. J.: Prentice-Hall. Inc., 1984).

3. Richard Wright, *Native Son* (New York: Harper & Row, 1940). All page references from this text appear in parentheses.

4. Richard Wright, *The Outsider* (New York: Harper & Row, 1953). All page references from this text appear in parentheses.

5. On the theme of the creative act of violence, see Richard E. Baldwin, "The Creative Vision of *Native Son*," *Massachusetts Review*, 14 (Spring 1973), 378–390; and Stephen B. Bennet and William W. Nichols, "Violence in Afro American Fiction: An Hypothesis," *Modern Fiction Studies*, 17 (Summer 1971), 221–228.

6. Siegel, 521.

7. Gibson, 729.

8. R. B. V. Larsen, "The Four Voices of Richard Wright's *Native Son*," *Negro American Literature Forum* (Winter 1972), 106.

9. Larsen, 105.

10. Richard Wright, *The Man Who Lived Underground*, in *Richard Wright Reader*, ed. Ellen Wright and Michel Fabre (New York: Harper & Row, 1978), 517–576. All page references from this text appear in parentheses.

11. Darwin Turner makes important comparisons between Bigger Thomas and Cross Damon in "*The Outsider*: Revision of an Idea," *College Language Association Journal*, 12 (June 1969), 310–321, but focuses primarily upon character, not on aspects of the narrative plan I describe here. The article is reprinted in *Richard Wright: A Collection of Critical Essays*, 163–172.

12. "How 'Bigger' Was Born," in *Native Son*, xvii.

13. Richard Wright, *American Hunger*. (New York: Harper & Row, 1944), 135. See also "I Tried to Be a Communist," *Atlantic Monthly*, Sept. 1944, 56, where a portion of *American Hunger* was printed.

14. *American Hunger*, 134.

Richard Wright's Struggles with Fathers

Elizabeth J. Ciner

> Be your own father . . .
> —*Invisible Man*

I

"If I were asked what is the one, over-all symbol or image gained from my living that most nearly represents what I feel to be the essence of American life," Richard Wright wrote in 1942, "I'd say it is that of a man struggling mightily . . . for self-possession" ("Why I Selected" 448). The struggle of the individual for self-possession, which is a struggle to be fully human and free, is the strongest unifying element in Wright's work. In his earliest published book, *Uncle Tom's Children*, Wright depicts ways in which black Americans are not externally free, writing about characters whose freedom to grow, live, work, and change is limited by whites. But already in that work he has begun to wonder about the possibility of achieving internal psychological freedom, especially for people who are oppressed. Although external freedom (or his characters' lack of it) continues to be a significant theme in Wright's work, by the time he publishes *Black Boy* in 1945 he has shifted his focus from the one to the other.

For Wright, internal freedom is contingent upon one's ability to make uncoerced choices. The internally free person is a self-assertive, self-controlled individual operating autonomously in the world. Not someone known by others ("The white South said it knew 'niggers,' and I was what the white South called a 'nigger,' Wright writes in *Black Boy* 283), not an object owned by another, the self-possessed person is his own master. And knowing who he is, the self-possessed person can look critically at (is not overwhelmed by) the society in which he finds himself, often taking the initiative needed to transform that society. To borrow language from Richard Shaull's introduction to *Pedagogy of the Oppressed*, the world for the free man is not, as it is for the slave, a "static and closed order, a *given* reality which man must accept and to which he must adjust" but rather "it is a problem to be worked on and solved" (12–13).

The form the struggle for self-possession most often takes in Wright's work is a struggle to achieve adulthood (or manhood, since all but one of Wright's protagonists are male), and there are both personal and historical reasons for this. Keneth Kinnamon isolates "four basic facts of Wright's youth—his racial status, his poverty, the disruption of his family, and his faulty education," all of which he claims "left ineradicable scars [on Wright's] psyche and deeply influenced his thought" as well as providing "much of the subject matter of his early writings" (4). Kinnamon's four basic facts, however, are aspects of a more general autobiographical fact which is that Wright saw himself as locked in combat with his family. Sometimes literally and more often metaphorically, Wright believed family members tried to beat and train out of him "a kind of consciousness, a mode of being that the way of life about [him] had said could not be, must not be" (187). In the autobiography Wright sees his relatives as enemies who, if they could, would choke off his desire to know, to do, to be, starving him not only physically but also intellectually, emotionally and spiritually.

Wright was clearest about his feelings towards his family in discussions on the autobiography. When he said, for instance, "I wrote the book to tell a series of incidents stringing through my childhood, but the main desire was to render a judgement on my environment" ("The Author" m3), he meant *his* environment. So little of the autobiography concerns itself with the white South that an understanding of Wright's critique of racism and of the white racist South depends on understanding not only what they, the whites, "do" to Richard, but also what his family does to Richard. Having accepted (for whatever reasons) the terms of racism, "the static and closed order," family members become accomplices of and agents for the State. Attempting to access the degree to which racism could and did damage human beings, Wright is not interested in cherishing but in exposing what lay at the heart of his own upbringing, the attempts of his family to prevent him from ever growing up.

Of course if Wright's family did not want him to be adult as he defined it, neither did the larger society. As Addison Gayle, Jr. points out, by the time of the Civil War, a "language system" had already evolved in America which "serve[d] the twin purposes of rationalizing slavery and binding the slave mentally to the slavocracy" (32). Both the rationalizing and the binding depended to a large degree on an analogy that equated black men and women with children. "Not content with merely enslaving black men, Americans undertook the task of stripping them of all semblance of humanity . . . reducing the man to the status of child" (4). The rationalizations were pristine in their simplicity: If black slaves were overgrown children, then white slave owners could pretend that no real loss of freedom had occurred; they were merely beneficent parents whose wayward children required constant supervision. Those slaves who did assert themselves, who were neither loyal nor tractable, who seemed indifferent or hostile to "parental" authority and guidance, were not men and women rebelling, convinced they were complete human beings whose rights even whites must respect, but rather boys and girls who had not yet learned their lessons, or dangerous beasts, savage children in grownups' bodies. Black people from this vantage point might be biologically adult, but they were not mature morally, intellectually, or socially. By definition, if you were black, you could not possibly act like an adult, and whites worked hard to make this definition a reality, punishing and redefining all acts of self-assertion.

Although clearly the legend sketched here is but one of a number of potent legends created about blacks by whites, it is one that, given his feelings about his own family, appealed to Wright. In some ways, this is what is most obvious about Wright's work. Throughout the fiction characters are blocked from reaching maturity. When they act like adults—when they try to protect their families, for instance, or improve their farms, or advance in their jobs—their actions are interpreted by whites as trying to "act white." The titles of Wright's first three published works, *Uncle Tom's Children, Native Son,* and *Black Boy,* contain references to non-adults; only posthumously do we find anything so positive as the title *Eight Men,* and even in that work the manhood of all but one of the characters is at issue. Black males are perpetually "boys" in the eyes of "the Man" in Wright's world. And to

be a boy is to be a "non-man," says Wright, a being "that knew
vaguely that it was human but felt that it was not" (*Black Boy* 213).

II

While it is certainly true, as Donald B. Gibson asserts, that the
"burden of the whole of the first chapter of *Black Boy* is a recital of
examples of parental rejection providing an explanation and a
justification for Wright's individualism" (493–494), it is also true that
while his family rejects him, Richard simultaneously rejects them.
Moreover, this dual rejection serves Richard: Resisting his family not
only teaches him in a general way to resist white racists (Gibson 497–
498), it also provides a specific map for him, a way out of the fate he
feels awaits him. Richard does not want anyone to dominate him—
black, white, parent, teacher, relative, boss, or priest. Committed to
ordering his life by his own feelings, he rejects his uncles, the school
principal, and Shorty. Above all others, though, he rejects his father
and his grandmother, the two people who in their opposite but to
Richard equally unacceptable reactions to racism, threaten him the
most. The one, his grandmother, finds solace in a stern religion she
tries to impose on Richard; the other, his father, deserts his family,
finding release in alcohol and adultery. Throughout the autobiography
Richard acts and reacts in ways which show him trying to be very
different from these two potential role models. In the end, by becoming
an author, Richard succeeds.

While the autobiography opens with an attack on his grandmother,
it is with Richard's father that much of the first long chapter is
concerned. Mr. Wright is "forbidding," the "lawgiver in the family," a
giant in front of whom Richard is awestruck. When Richard's family
moves to Memphis, Richard, afraid to go into the strange city streets
alone, is confined to home where he must be quiet while his father (a
night porter) sleeps. One morning Richard finds himself forced to quiet
a kitten whose mewing provokes his father. "'Kill the damn thing . . .
Do anything, but get it away from here'" (17), his father commands.
Immediately resentful, Richard hangs the kitten and so, Wright tells us,
enjoys his "first triumph" (18) over his father.

When Richard had hanged the kitten, his mother had warned him
"'That kitten's going to get you'" (18), a warning Richard shrugged off,
saying "'That kitten can't even breathe now'" (18). But Richard learns he

is wrong: "My mother's words," he reports, "made it live again in my mind" (20). Victim here of another's language, Richard experiences words as weapons, as surely as he will experience them fourteen years later when reading Mencken. As a final gesture, his mother forces him into a prayer of forgiveness—"Dear God, our father, forgive me, for I knew not what I was doing"—which perhaps for the first time links biological and spiritual fathers. Subsequent episodes will cement the connection: When Richard complains of hunger, his mother insists that he will have to wait for God to send food because his father is gone; a preacher, "God's representative," a man also used to having his "own way" (33), eats all the fried chicken while Richard labors unsuccessfully to finish his soup. Fathers, spiritual or biological, Richard's experience leads him to believe, satisfy their own appetites at the expense of their children.

With his father gone, Richard's mother sends him out to buy the groceries. Richard sets out "proud" and feeling "like a grownup" (13). When he is robbed and beaten (and forced out of the house by his mother), he compensates for his youth and small size, arming himself with a big stick, defending himself first against the boys who stole from him and then against their parents who "rushed into the streets and threatened [him]: They had never seen such frenzy. For the first time in my life I shouted at grownups, telling them I would give them the same if they bothered me." Richard's victory here is a multiple one. Supplanting his father as provider of food, he triumphs over him a second time and more decisively. At the same time he triumphs over his own fear. Where Richard had been "afraid to go into the city streets alone" (16) now he has "won" for himself the "right to the streets of Memphis" (25).

Once free from fear, Richard quickly familiarizes himself with the adult world which has captured his father, showing himself to be his father's son. Far from home, the boy frequents a saloon, learns to drink, and is taught to proposition women. At the age of six, "[f]or a penny or a nickel I would repeat to anyone whatever was whispered to me," encouraged by the responses he got. "In my foggy, tipsy state, the reaction of the men and women to my mysterious words enthralled me. I ran from person to person, laughing, hiccoughing, spewing out filth that made them bend double with glee" (29). Given his inclinations, why Wright does not follow in his father's footsteps is one of the mysteries of the text. Perhaps his mother's beatings are effective.

Perhaps when the effects of the alcohol wear off what Richard
remembers from these experiences is not the comfort of the drink but
the power of his socially unacceptable language.

Richard sees his father one last time in boyhood, at the home of
his father's mistress. He recoils from the encounter for reasons he
cannot make clear to himself:

> We left. I had the feeling that I had had to do with something
> unclean. Many times in the years after that the image of my
> father and the strange woman, their faces lit by the dancing
> flames, would surge up in my imagination so vivid and strong
> that I felt I could reach out and touch it; I would stare at it,
> feeling that it possessed some vital meaning which always
> eluded me. (42)

According to Albert Stone, the fire "represents the sexual passion which
separates and unites father, mother, and mistress and which likewise
includes the child who, looking into the coals, sees himself an
unconscious participant in the sexual drama" (131). But as a child, all
Richard knows is that he is on one side of a room, his father is on the
other, between them is "a bright fire that blazed in a grate" (40), and the
gap between them is not as wide as Richard would have it be. Even not
knowing what other life is possible for him, Richard instinctively
rejects the narrow and degraded life his father has chosen.

Carl Brignano claims that Wright was searching for a father and
that the search "was a real one," although symbolically the search
expresses itself as " a search for Negro dignity, economic opportunity,
and social acceptance in a racially integrated South" (6). More to the
point perhaps, Wright appears to be searching for a way to be a father, a
person in power if not over others than at least over himself. His
father's fire attracts Richard, but his father's life, finally, does not.
Wright is emphatic on this point in the chapter's final paragraphs:

> A quarter of a century was to elapse between the time when I
> saw my father sitting with the strange woman and the time I
> was to see him again . . . a sharecropper, clad in ragged
> overalls, holding a muddy hoe in his gnarled, veined hands—a
> quarter of a century during which my mind and consciousness
> had become so greatly and violently altered that when I tried to
> talk to him I realized that, though ties of blood made us kin,

though I could see a shadow of my face in his face, though there was an echo of my voice in his voice, we were forever strangers, speaking a different language, living on vastly distant planes of reality. (42)

Whatever Wright has become it is not his father. From this point in the narrative, the older Wright drops out, his ghost, so to speak, emerging at the end of *Black Boy* to haunt Richard when he returns to Memphis as a young man. Memphis, for Wright, is the city his father "had gone to . . . seeking life" (43). But his father "had failed in the city; a black peasant whose life had been hopelessly snarled in the city, and who had at last fled the city" (43), that same city in whose "burning arms" Richard is "lifted" and "borne . . . toward alien and undreamed-of shores of knowing" (43).

With Richard's father out of the picture, his grandmother becomes head of the family and the authority figure Richard must contend with on a day-to-day basis. She is a religious woman, a fanatic Seventh Day Adventist, according to Wright, and from the very beginning her religiousness conflicts with Richard's free expression: "I was dreaming of running and playing and shouting," the first paragraph of the autobiography goes, "but the vivid image of Granny's old, white, wrinkled, grim face, framed by a halo of tumbling black hair . . . made me afraid" (9). Richard finally gets out of the house by burning it down, and, while Richard is not labelled a Devil proper until the scenes which come at the end of the second chapter, there is an unmistakably diabolical aspect to his "play" in the opening scene; at least part of him clearly wants to see his grandmother lying helpless upon her bed, "yellow flames" instead of that halo in her hair. The motivation behind Richard's act, his characterization of Granny as an awe-inspiring figure lying somewhere above him, and his attraction to fire, all raise the question of Richard's own affiliation with Satan. Richard is first fascinated by the liveliness of the fire; as a result of his play with it, he falls into a fever and feels his body on fire. Perhaps, in his misbehavior, he finds a way to incorporate this living vital element within him. But if Richard is a devil, then he is one in the romantic sense, a rebel and heretic defying not lawful authority but tyrannical oppression. Not unlike Prometheus, Richard steals fire and uses it in ways objected to strenuously by those in authority.

After his father's desertion, Richard, his brother, and his mother return to Granny's house. There Richard meets the young schoolteacher

Ella who boards with the family. When he asks her about the books she reads, Ella, who knows Granny forbids novels, attempts to placate Richard by closing her book and whispering to him *Bluebeard and His Seven Wives*. Richard is "[e]nchanted and enthralled" by the story. "My imagination blazed" (47), Wright writes. But just as Ella is about to finish, "when my interest was keenest, when I was lost to the world around me" (47), Granny steps out on the porch and puts an end to the story, telling Ella, "'I want none of that Devil stuff in my house!'" (47), warning Richard, "'You're going to burn in hell'" (48).

The story is indeed the Devil's stuff, about Bluebeard, a satanic figure if ever there was one, and it is precisely the story Richard wants to hear: "Ella's whispered story of deception and murder had been the first experience in my life that had elicited from me a total emotional response" (48). Richard's life is given symbolic form through the story; deprived of it he is deprived of a way to come to grips with his life through literature. But as the subsequent scene shows, Richard not only empathizes with Bluebeard's wives but also with Bluebeard who through deception and violence achieves his unlawful desires. Within days, Richard mounts an ingenious attack on Granny, this one a symbolic and linguistic assault.

Richard and his brother are taking baths in two tubs of water under the watchful eyes of Granny. Splashing water, flinging suds at one another, they ignore Granny's scolding until she puts down her knitting and calls Richard to her:

> "Bend over," she ordered.
> I stooped and she scrubbed my anus. My mind was in a sort of daze, midway between daydreaming and thinking. Then, before I knew it, words—words whose meaning I did not fully know—had slipped out of my mouth.
> "When you get through, kiss back there," I said, the words rolling softly but unpremeditately. (49)

Pandemonium ensues. With eyes "blazing," Granny shoves Richard from her and beats him with a towel she is holding. Naked, he runs screaming from the house as his mother hurries from her bed. Granny, close to hysterics, reports on what "that black little Devil" (50) has done, and Richard's mother takes up both towel and chase.

Much in the form of this scene looks back to the opening scene of the autobiography; its content, though, derives from Richard's early experiences with language: words like "enthralled" and "dazed" recall his saloon experiences while "soap" and "scrub" attach themselves to an episode which involved Richard scribbling obscene words on windows with a soap cake. None of the characters makes any of these connections. Granny's explanation holds sway: She "said emphatically that she knew who had ruined me," Richard reports, "that she knew I learned about 'foul practices' from reading Ella's books."

Granny, who distrusts stories because they are fictions and hence lies is wrong about Ella and foul practices only in fact. Fictionally speaking Granny is right; stories can be the Devil's work and this one has been, providing Richard with what he needed to attack Granny for interfering with his pleasure in hearing the story. While Richard called the story one of deception and murder, it is also a story of sexual perversion, of foul practices.

When Richard says that Granny "knew who had ruined" him by teaching him "foul practices," the implication is clearly sexual, and Wright is effecting a comic reversal with Ella becoming the seducer and Richard the one seduced. The language of the Bluebeard scene itself is sexual—feelings well up, things seem to throb, Richard feels his body ablaze with excitement. Referring back to the word-play Richard indulged in in the first chapter, this language also recalls Richard's encounter with his father and the strange woman, the incident he came away from feeling as if he had had something "to do with something unclean" (42). Richard's choice of a sexual gesture towards Granny and Wright's adoption of sexually laden language in the description of Richard's responses to literature show Richard open to the same kinds of impulses his father is open to. But Richard will channel those impulses differently, the differentness demonstrating his discontinuity with his father. Initiated as he is in the Bluebeard scene not into the world of the flesh but into the world of story-telling, Richard's impulses serve another god.

Richard's responses to the story are not unlike the responses of an initiate, a convert, and they parallel Granny's responses to religion. Where she sees angels, he sees magical presences. His books generate in him a transcendent experience and momentarily blot out reality, making him feel "lost to reality" and so compete with her religion in which she feels dead to the world. Richard in fact adopts his grandmother's terms—devil, evil, hell—and then transforms them. From Granny's point of view, the dreamy schoolteacher is "evil," books are the "devil's stuff," Richard's desire to know, "the devil's work," and Richard himself "a little black devil" who surely is "going to burn in hell." That is all right with Richard, who appropriates the terms; he "burns to learn to read novels" (49) and "tortures his mother" as a good devil ought "to define every strange word" he comes upon, because he has learned from Granny (as surely as Frederick Douglass learned from Captain Auld) that words are the "gateway to a forbidden and enchanting land" (49).

In the course of *Black Boy* what is implicit in the Bluebeard-bathtub sequence is made explicit: if Richard is a devil, then the saint is someone who has cut him or her self off from life; if his acts are evil, then being good is akin to being dead; if he is headed for hell, then heaven is a static place where nothing much happens. Within this framework, novels *are* the devil's work, opening up possibilities for the individual in a society which depends for its existence on those possibilities being denied, a society, furthermore, which works to deny that any life other than that proscribed is possible.

Richard's reaction to this proscription is complex and germinal. At the age of twelve, having promised Granny "to pray hard," Richard goes up to his room every afternoon, "but everything I could think of saying seemed silly." Failing even at writing hymn verses, Richard claims that "the Holy Ghost was simply nowhere near me" (132). The Holy Ghost may be absent, but not so Richard's muse: "One day while killing my hour of prayer" (132), Wright writes, he is inspired to write an Indian love story. "I had made something," he writes, "no matter how bad it was; and it was mine" (133). Paradoxically, then, Richard's first work of art emerges under the pressure of Granny's religiosity. As if he had taken his directions from her, Richard creates not prayer but exactly the kind of work Granny burns, becoming exactly what she had feared he would become.

If the crucial difference between Richard and his father has been that the son succumbs not to passion but to art, then the difference between Richard and his grandmother is that while she uses religion to withdraw from a world she finds intolerable, he will seek a way through words, as Wright would put it, to alter his relationship to his environment and thereby prove himself to be a free man. From Richard's point of view, Granny and others like her fly to religion as an answer to the pain of their existence. He flees the South, however, so that he may find the words to describe the life he has known, and in describing that life create for himself (and for others) a new one. Writing stories is finally a religious activity for Richard, writing redeeming him as religion redeems Granny. While Granny's religion frees her from the world, Richard's frees him into it.

His choice of professions, then, is no accident: becoming a writer, he becomes at once an author, creator, and artist, and this may be said to specifically solve his problems. As a writer of books, he creates new worlds and thereby competes with Granny's God, the source of her authority and Richard's spiritual father; as an autobiographer, he engenders himself and so displaces his biological father. Recreating his world and himself for us, as he sees it, Wright even outwits his political fathers, white men of the South, who never imagine a black boy *could* become a writer. Wright does become one though, and in so doing transforms himself, permanently altering his fate and status. No longer a native son doomed to an obscure and deadened existence, he becomes Richard Wright.

References

Brignano, Carl. *Richard Wright: An Introduction to the Man and His Work.* Pittsburgh, Pa.: University of Pittsburgh Press, 1970.

Gayle, Addison, Jr. *The Way of the World.* Garden City, N.Y.: Doubleday, 1976.

Gibson, Donald B. "Richard Wright and the Trauma of Autobiographical Rebirth." *Callaloo,* 9 (1986): 492–498.

Kinnamon, Keneth. *The Emergence of Richard Wright: A Study in Literature and Society.* Urbana: University of Illinois Press, 1972.

Shaull, Richard. Introduction, *Pedagogy of the Oppressed,* by Paulo Friere. Trans. Myra Bergman Ramos. New York: The Seabury Press, 1968.

Stone, Albert E. *Autobiographical Occasions and Original Acts.* Philadelphia: University of Pennsylvania Press, 1982.

Wright, Richard. "The Author Meets the Critics." New York radio interview, printed in *PM's Sunday Picture News*, Magazine Section, April 15, 1945, m3.

―――. *Black Boy.* New York: Harper & Row, 1945.

―――. "Why I Selected 'How "Bigger" Was Born.'" *This Is My Best.* Ed. Whit Burnett. Philadelphia: Blackiston & Grayson, 1942.

Why "Bigger" Lives On:
Student Reaction to *Native Son*

Paul Newlin

The July 14, 1986, issue of *Newsweek* features a cover showing the Statue of Liberty, flood-lit against a foreground of rocketing fireworks, and under the banner title of the magazine in print even larger than the title itself is the one-word caption "Wow!" As fate, the timing of publishing weekly magazines, and the calendar would have it, *Newsweek's* feature coverage of the centennial celebration of the Statue of Liberty appeared on Bastille Day—another French connection redolent with slogans of liberty, equality, and fraternity; but the "wows" of fireworks, good feelings, and romantic notions of individual freedoms choke in one's throat as you leaf through the magazine to its first page of substance, page 5, and the "Periscope" section. Here, under a photograph of a pamphlet's cover is a news story headed "Colorblind" which reports on a Federal Bureau of Investigation *Law Enforcement Bulletin* whose subject is "Rape: The Dangers of Providing Confrontational Advice."

The pamphlet cover displayed is the June 1986 issue of the *FBI Law Enforcement Bulletin* and it shows the left forearm and hand of a white female, complete with wedding band on the third finger. Gripping the wrist of the white female arm is a right black hand, which is larger, more muscular and undoubtedly male. The illustration was clear: rape in America is symbolized by a black male assaulting a white, married female, who, with her wedding band less-than-obliquely suggests defiled motherhood. The Assistant Director of the FBI noted that after a "handful" of the copies of the bulletin were distributed, and as soon as he saw it, he "knew it could be considered racially insulting" and had the bulletin withdrawn at a cost of $15,000 and re-issued with a new cover depicting two white arms and hands.[1]

The irony of virtually the first news story in the Statue of Liberty issue of a national news magazine depicting racial bigotry of the country's federal law-enforcement agency sent me back to Richard Wright's recounting of how the plot for *Native Son* formed itself; in his essay "How 'Bigger' Was Born," Wright says:

> The moment I began to write, the plot fell out, so to speak. I'm not trying to oversimplify or make the process seem oversubtle. At bottom what happened is very easy to explain. Any Negro . . . knows that times without number he has heard of some Negro boy being picked up on the streets and carted off to jail and charged with "rape." This thing happens so often that to my mind it had become a representative symbol of the Negro's uncertain position in America.[2]

The trumped-up charge of rape of a white woman by a black man is so pervasive in post Civil War society as to clearly validate Wright's claim of its being a representative symbol of black Americans' uncertain position in this country. The year following the publication of *Native Son*, J. W. Cash published the trenchant *The Mind of the South,* in which he places the "rape complex" following the Civil War into a context that lays some of the blame for this racist mania at the feet of northern hate mongers. Cash's study and more recent sociohistorical accounts that bear on this topic, such as Calvin Hernton's *Sex and Racism in America* (1966) and Angela Davis' *Women, Race, and Class* (1981) are but a representative sampling of abundant evidence to support Wright's contention in "How 'Bigger' Was Born." Almost a half-century after Wright wrote those words, the profundity of his experiences and observations have lost no weight—rape still is a representative symbol of black Americans' uncertain position in this country.[3]

For nearly half of that half-century, I have been teaching *Native Son* on a fairly regular basis to predominantly white, middle-class, college students at state universities in the Northeast. My motives in assigning *Native Son* have been twofold: first of all, it is a powerful, first-rate novel by an influential black American writer, and my students' exposure to the book would not likely take place outside the academy; second, it illustrates a culmination of the naturalistic school in America. Whatever my motives, the results have been uniformly the same: the students have been shocked, sobered, and put into a reflective mood as by no other novel I have taught, and it has taken the contemporary tangible racism of the FBI to jolt me into attempting to analyze in this paper my students' responses—something I have reflected upon sporadically over the years of my involvement as reader and teacher with Bigger Thomas.

Often, as part of a course-evaluation questionnaire, I will ask students to list the one work on our syllabus of late-nineteenth, early-twentieth century American literature that affected them the most—be the effect emotional, aesthetic, whatever. *Native Son* regularly leads the works selected by a large margin, and when I have quizzed the students further about their choice, the responses I get reflect much of Wright's intentions in writing the book. For instance, in "How 'Bigger' Was Born," Wright in commenting on the reception of his earlier work, *Uncle Tom's Children*, says:

> I realized that I had made an awfully naive mistake. I found that I had written a book which even banker's daughters could read and weep over and feel good about. I swore to myself that if I ever wrote another book, no one would weep over it; that it would be so hard and deep that they would have to face it without the consolation of tears.[4]

Certainly the murder of Bessie goes a long way toward preventing bankers' daughters' tears of sympathy for Bigger. Bessie's bludgeoning was no accident—it was a horrific naturalistic touch of Wright's to make the comparison of Mary's death with that of Dreiser's Roberta in *An American Tragedy* a moot point. The grisly scene of Bigger smashing the sleeping Bessie's head and face with a brick makes the most calloused reader squirm—it is, in Wright's words, a "hard" scene foreshadowed by the opening scene of the novel in which Bigger in his one-room tenement flat confronts the rat.

Wright acknowledges the great difficulty he had in developing the opening scene, but Wright has framed *Native Son* with scenes that force the reader to face Bigger Thomas in the context of Bigger's exclusion from even the mere hint of the possibility of liberty, equality and fraternity. The opening sequence with the rat leads towards the novel's conclusion with no suggestion of a positive resolution. Wright explains:

I ended it just as I had begun it, showing Bigger living
dangerously, taking his life into his hands, accepting what life
had made him. The lawyer, Max, was placed in Bigger's cell at
the end of the novel to register the moral—or what I felt was
the moral—horror of Negro life in the United States.[5]

There is much talk these days of a return to capital punishment
nationwide, and many of the students I have taught profess support of
an Old Testament philosophy of "an eye for an eye and a tooth for a
tooth." Yet when I have asked them if they think Bigger should have
been executed, not a single student has agreed—even when reminded
about Bessie. "Why not?" I ask. "If you think that a person who kills
someone should in turn be killed, why not Bigger?" The answer
received is always a variation of the simple judgment: "It just isn't
fair." And therein rests the profound strength of this novel.

What is implicit in *Native Son* for students is a clear statement
that much of what is ingrained in them as Americans—all Americans—
is leached out, eroded, ultimately denied in Bigger's black ghetto
experience. For most students this is a revelation that runs counter to
the truisms of their education and the pomp and ritual of a self-
consciously patriotic society. Life is *not* fair if you are Bigger
Thomas—it never was, and never will be, and "the horror of Negro life
in America" that ultimately disillusions the naive idealism of lawyer
Max's doctrinaire, romantic communism hits the apolitical, middle-
class, good-kid, college student right between the eyes.

Nationalism for most white Americans sometimes seems no more
than a knee-jerk arrogance that we are infallible because, after all, don't
our coins say "In God We Trust" on them? The basis for such
jingoistic co-opting of God rests on the notion of Manifest Destiny.
For a country expanding west in the nineteenth century (stealing the
land from its native occupants and despoiling nature), this expansion
was seen somehow to fit into God's plan: white European-Americans
were the self-proclaimed chosen people, and the material success of the
western expansion proved them to be infallibly in league with God.
Paradoxically, at the same time that Manifest Destiny was being
articulated, the transcendentalism of Emerson and Theodore Parker
embraced a faith in a moral law inherent in nature and celebrated the
capacity of perceiving and responding to what all recognized as just and
proper human behavior; the strength of this faith rests in the intuitive
recognition of fair play as a natural condition of human harmony. Fair

play, thus, is a given quality of the American psyche that appears to be almost genetically rooted. However, this is not to say that my college students, prior to their exposure to the world of Bigger Thomas, are naive to the other side of the paradox: exploitation for material gain. On the contrary, they are very aware of the great segment of American life that succeeds by deception and stealth: American Big Business. But in regards to Big Business, they know who the enemy is, and they accept *caveat emptor* as a condition of the game—a sorry condition, a sometimes humorous condition, but a condition one can combat if given the opportunity. In *Native Son* they see that Bigger has no opportunity of choice and thus no way to combat the cheating aspect of what for Bigger is anything but *free* enterprise.

Bigger's lack of identity with national traditions of fair play is put into the broad context by Wright, who imagines a generic Bigger saying: "Man, what we need is a leader like Marcus Garvey. We need a nation, a flag, an army of our own. We colored folks ought to organize into groups and have generals, lieutenants. . . . We ought to take Africa and have a national home." Wright goes on to comment on these words of his imagined spokesman:

> Those words told me that the civilization which had given birth to Bigger contained no spiritual sustenance, had created no culture which could hold and claim his allegiance and faith, had sensitized him and had left him stranded, a free agent to roam the streets of our cities, a hot and whirling vortex of undisciplined and unchannelized impulses.[6]

In calling Bigger a "free agent," Wright mocks the meaning of free, and ironically produces a figure whose literary heritage was heroic: the independent American in isolation—Natty Bumppo, Melville's Ishmael, Huck Finn. The only thing that Bigger has in common with those figures whose heroism rests on their rejection of society and the independence of their spirits, is their isolation: theirs by choice, his by the circumstance of the color of his skin and urban birth.

Bigger, then, is the first American urban *isolato*, and he differs from Ralph Ellison's isolated Invisible Man in that the latter was an urban dweller by both circumstance and choice; and though limited by his invisibleness, he has the flexibility of mobility. Bigger's problem is one of black visibility from the very beginning. While the Invisible Man's lament has the touchstone of Louis Armstrong's bone-deep plaintive refrain of "What did I do to be so black and blue," Bigger's questioning finds no consoling blues line in its bitter call for fair play. Bigger is trapped by his black color and by his white aspirations— aspirations that historically had no application to black Americans. Wright viewed Bigger's aspirations this way:

> . . . there was that American part of Bigger which is the heritage of us all, that part of him which we get from our seeing and hearing, from school, from the hopes and dreams of our friends; that part of him which the common people of America never talk of but take for granted. Among millions of people the deepest convictions of life are never discussed openly; they are felt, implied, hinted at tacitly and obliquely in their hopes and fears. We live by an idealism that makes us believe that the Constitution is a good document of government, that the Bill of Rights is a good legal and humane principle to safeguard our civil liberties, that every man and woman should have the opportunity to realize himself, to seek his own individual fate and goal, his own peculiar and untranslatable destiny. I don't say that Bigger knew this in the terms in which I'm speaking of it; I don't say that any such thought ever entered his head. His emotional and intellectual life was never that articulate. But he knew it emotionally, intuitively, for his emotions and his desires were developed, and he caught it, as most of us do, from the mental and emotional climate of our times. Bigger had all of this in him, dammed up, buried, implied, and I had to develop it in fictional form.[7]

Wright's success in showing this aspect of Bigger seen against the "heritage of us all" is especially effective for college-age readers. Students extending their formal education beyond high school, though their professed statements and actions often outwardly belie it, tacitly accept a civic responsibility for maintaining the heritage Wright describes. Thus, when Wright forges an image of Bigger in a society that denies this heritage and makes that denial appear as Bigger's inevitable fate, ambivalences by the reader concerning that heritage just as inevitably arise. A true disciple of the naturalistic school of fiction, Wright says that he wrote "with the conviction in mind that the main burden of all serious fiction consists almost wholly of character-destiny and the items, social, political, and personal of that character-destiny."[8] Bigger's "character-destiny" is foreshadowed in the opening scene when his introduction to the reader is seen in the context of a symbolic beginning. The morning begins in a routine fashion with the household arising at the sound of an alarm clock, but the scene holds little domestic identity beyond that common sound for the reader who learns that a predatory foot-long rat is also part of the dawning of a new day and that the rat's appearance is no rarity. "There he is again, Bigger!" screams Bigger's mother, and a graphic battle to the rat's death ensues with Bigger smashing the rat with an iron skillet and then hysterically shouting "You sonofabitch!" as he pounds the rat's skull with a shoe. No blue-steel revolver or stiletto nor even a Saturday-night special or switchblade is the instrument of death, rather a skillet and a shoe—two items of abject domesticity turned into the means of death and vengeance. It is just this incongruous and terrifyingly homely touch to this scene of violence and vulnerability that sets the tone for Bigger's destiny.

In a world where senseless violence and terrorism have become a staple of the evening television news, college students still are brought up short and pale at Bigger's encounter with the rat, because it has no place in the "heritage of us all." And though, in the fine tradition of American heroic fiction, Bigger does dispatch his evil adversary, the victory does not free his spirit, allow him unshackled entrance into the independence and opportunities of the frontier, or restore law and order with the promise of ongoing tranquility; instead, his heroism is so desperate, slight, and self-conscious, that in his own emotional release from tension he perversely teases his sister with the dead rat's body, an action which leads in turn to devastation in his ultimate rejection when his mother angrily renounces him with: "Bigger, sometimes I wonder why I birthed you." Bigger's character is established in this scene; his destiny will follow suit.

Although Wright set out to compose a novel so hard that it would deny tears over the fate of the victims, he claims consciously to have then worked in a guilt theme after completing the first draft. By implication, he acknowledges that guilt was hinted at in the first draft, and it seems impossible to me that it was not there from the establishment of Bigger's character-destiny in the scene with the rat. Wright doesn't elaborate on *who* is guilty for *what* in "How 'Bigger' Was Born," but guilt is part of "the heritage of us all" and need not be spelled out except when it plays a dramatic purpose, as it does with Jan's and Mary's pathetic attempts at expiation in their uneasy gestures at brotherhood. Guilt is everywhere—from Mrs. Thomas' cruel questioning of why she brought Bigger into this world, Mrs. Dalton's collective guilt as a symbolic representation of a blind, self-praising, affluent white society, and Bigger's own irascible bullying of his street pals in an effort to assuage his fears, to Max's appalled recognition of what Wright called the moral of the novel: "the horror of Negro life in the United States."

The reader, and especially the young reader whose innocence and sense of fair play is also "the heritage of us all," feels increasingly guilty and miserable as Bigger's fear, flight, and fate unfold. Yet, intuitively that reader knows Wright was again correct in his appraisal of his readership and his society when he claims in reference to that guilt-ridden reader that "this same average citizen, with his kindness, his American sportsmanship and good will, would probably act with the mob if a self-respecting Negro family moved into his apartment building to escape the Black Belt and its terrors and limitations."[9] In the half-century since Wright wrote those words the only updating they would need would be the addition of the words "or suburbs" after "apartment building."

All of the things I have mentioned are part of the experience in some degree or other of my students, but I think that as students of literature they feel an added dimension of lawyer Max's horror. At the very end of *Native Son*, Bigger says to Max: "What I killed for, I *am*! . . . What I killed for must've been good! . . . When a man kills, it's for something, things hard enough to kill for 'em. . . . It's the truth Mr. Max." This is "the horror of Negro life" that Wright speaks about in his essay, and it is so far removed from the sociopolitical view of Max's world that he is speechless and draws back from human contact with Bigger, leaving the latter in ultimate isolation as the result of his epiphany about the killing he has done. Wright has fulfilled his envisioned character-destiny for Bigger, but the horror of Bigger's interpretation of Mary's death and Bessie's murder transcends the scientific and environmental determinism of naturalistic ideologies in that it becomes for Bigger an aesthetic act—an accomplishment of creation; and the added horror of murder as an example of the sublime makes Poe's elevation of the death of a beautiful woman to that of "the most poetical topic in the world" seem genteel indeed. Or, as Wright observes at the conclusion of "How 'Bigger' Was Born":

> . . . we . . . do have in the Negro the embodiment of a past
> tragic enough to appease the spiritual hunger of even a [Henry]
> James; and we have in the oppression of the Negro a shadow
> athwart our national life dense and heavy enough to satisfy even
> the gloomy broodings of a Hawthorne. And if Poe were alive,
> he would not have to invent horror; horror would invent him.[10]

The horror of which Richard Wright wrote in 1940 still infuses
Native Son today. In telling us how Bigger was born, Wright has also
told us why Bigger lives on. One can make a strong case that "the
horror of Negro life in the United States" has diminished since Bigger
was born in 1940. Yet black youngsters still wake up to battle rats or
worse in ever-enlarging black urban ghettoes, and though Bigger and
Gus currently could sit undisturbed in the orchestra of Chicago's movie
houses, one need look no further than the June 1986 *FBI Law
Enforcement Bulletin* to know how Bigger's presence in Mary Dalton's
bedroom would be interpreted in Chicago today. Bigger Thomas'
position in the literary canon of twentieth-century American literature is
secure precisely because rape remains "the representative symbol of the
Negro's uncertain position in America." Passage of time modifies
heritage but slowly, and the fear, the guilt, the horror of Wright's
Native Son infuses each generation of readers with its moral: "the
horror of Negro life in the United States." Is there any wonder my
students are affected by *Native Son* as by no other book I teach?

Notes

1. "Periscope," *Newsweek* (July 14, 1986), 5.
2. Richard Wright, "How 'Bigger' Was Born," *Native Son*, Perennial
   Classic edition (New York: Harper and Row, 1966), xxviii.
3. See particularly: Chapter I, Book Two, "Of the Frontier the
   Yankee Made" in Cash's *The Mind of The South* (New York,
   1941); Chapter One, "The Sexualization of Racism," and Chapter
   Four, "The Negro Male" in Hernton's *Sex and Racism in America*
   (New York, 1966); and Chapter 11, "Rape, Racism and the Myth
   of the Black Rapist" in Davis' *Women, Race and Class* (New York,
   1981).
4. Ibid., xxvii.
5. Ibid., xxxiii.

6. Ibid., xix.
7. Ibid., xxv.
8. Ibid., xxxi.
9. Ibid., xxix.
10. Ibid., xxxiv.

A Political Vision of Afro-American Culture: Richard Wright's "Bright and Morning Star"

Thomas Larson

Richard Wright wrote *Uncle Tom's Children* in the late 1930s when he was an active member of the Communist Party of the United States. There were two editions of the book: the first contained four novellas which won *Story Magazine*'s WPA short story contest in 1938. The later edition added "The Ethics of Living Jim Crow" as a preface and "Bright and Morning Star" as the fifth story. Since some of the stories had communist protagonists and Wright was a Party member, the Party was deeply interested in Wright's portrayal. Their reaction in the press was mostly positive. Granville Hicks had problems with the stories' narrative structures (161), and Alan Calmer said the novellas did not "dig down" deep enough into the class or economic causes of Afro-American suffering (7). Two later critics have countered Calmer's notion, arguing that Wright made Party interests secondary, because he stressed racial differences over those of economic disparity. Marcus Klein believed that "the book did dig down so far as to undermine the Party position, precisely by dealing in representations in black and white" (*Foreigners* 283). Edward Margolies saw a dichotomy between Party interests about the class struggle and the way Wright viewed them. "Communists are viewed in a kindly light . . . but they are only remotely instrumental in effecting his heroes' discovery of themselves and their world. . . . Wright's simple Negro peasants [in the last three stories of the later edition] arrive at their sense of self-realization by applying basic Christian principles to the situations in which they find themselves" (Hakutani 129).

Of all the stories, "Bright and Morning Star" holds the most tension between race and revolution because its vision of violence encourages both a care for and a sacrifice of human life. The story centers on Aunt Sue, an old black woman, who has had one son arrested for communist organizing activities and feels she will lose her other son, Johnny-Boy, in the same way. Since the family are all Party members (the father has died) and since she must protect the clandestine meetings Johnny-Boy and his fellow comrades hold, she must fend off a gang of whites who use the excuse of quashing subversive activity in order to brutalize the radicals. Aunt Sue is devoted to her son, and she is more than pleased that he has found happiness with Reva, a trustworthy white woman. At the same time, his political activity is crucial to her. She has come to have faith in the goals of communism, so she protects the anonymity of Johnny-Boy and his friends. The events in the story dramatically contrast Aunt Sue's love for her sons, Reva, and her son's comrades with the whites' brutal murder of Aunt Sue and Johnny-Boy in the end.

The outcome of the story hinges on Aunt Sue's "betrayal" of the Party when she mistakenly gives a white man, Booker, information about a Party meeting. Momentarily setting aside her habit of distrusting whites, she tells Booker the truth because he convinces her he is a comrade. But he turns out to be a stool pigeon for the Sheriff. Her failure to distrust him, however, has ironical significance because events in the story turn her action into a positive contribution to the Party. But more significantly, Aunt Sue learns that her active distrust was part of her cultural response, a survivalist tactic whereby she is able to protect herself from the harassment of whites.

By revealing the character of trust and betrayal inherent in Afro-American culture, Wright echoes an idea about black and white conflict and dependence central to the thinking of many black social philosophers and writers, among them W.E.B. DuBois and, later, James Baldwin. In the South at the turn of the century (a South that Wright knew intimately), DuBois argued in *The Souls of Black Folk* that Afro-Americans' vision of themselves and, consequently, their survival in a hostile world were attributable to a "double-consciousness, [a] sense of always looking at one's self through the eyes of others" (16–17). Of course, the "others" were the whites who controlled that vision. In attempting to dismantle the other's control, one which had kept individual blacks from being "both a Negro and an American" and then from merging those two selves into one, DuBois said that deception was a natural part of the culture, that "the South used it for many years against its conquerors [and] to-day [1903] it must be prepared to see its black proletariat turn that same two-edged weapon against itself" (150). In fact, DuBois saw "deception and flattery . . . cajoling and lying" as often the only effective means of fighting oppression, where oppression was a much greater crime he felt than any means blacks used to oppose it. That these tactics were held by whites as somehow inherent to blacks' character, in effect victimizing them with their own methods of survival, hardly bears repeating.

James Baldwin, writing in *The Fire Next Time* just two years after Richard Wright's death in 1960, attacked the concept that blacks somehow had to become equal to whites, to raise themselves up to a level that "in the white man's public or private life" assumed some standard "that one should desire to imitate" (128). Who would wish, Baldwin wrote, to imitate *these* oppressors, especially as they have "projected onto the Negro" their own fears and suspicions. But though white people for Baldwin have consistently betrayed their own promises (and the insulting tardiness of the 1954 Brown decision confirms this), a genuine trust of whites must still arise in the black community. Conceived miraculously it seems, only a reasoned response to white power can lead blacks towards a clear vision of themselves and thereby forestall the coming fire. Writing to his nephew James on the eve of the urban revolt he sensed in 1962, Baldwin instructs him about the "terrible paradox" that whites have "constructed to make you believe what [they] say about you." "There is no reason for you to try to become like white people and there is no basis whatever for their impertinent assumption that *they* must accept *you*. The really terrible thing, old buddy, is that *you* must accept *them*" (19). For centuries, Afro-Americans have had to trust whites both to explore the few freedoms given them by whites in power and to regain control when the manipulation of any trust inherent in those freedoms threatened their lives.

Richard Wright grew up with the psychological factors before him DuBois had outlined, and I am certain Wright would have agreed with Baldwin's later assertions about acceptance and integration. Yet in identifying how racial consciousness was based in these perversions of trust, Wright saw it all in the 1930s a little differently: his fiction of this period reveals that a deep awareness of the consciousness of Afro-

American life will compel revolutionary political action and therefore be the next step for radicals in America to take. Wright's self-appointed role was to make explicit in fiction a testament to the coercion of whites and the mutability of the black response. I believe that "Bright and Morning Star" exposes the antagonism within the pathological system of trust and betrayal to show first and most importantly, that this system is at the heart of Afro-American identity. The story also announces to the Party that it should embrace the fullest view of race-consciousness possible, one particularly conscious of the paradoxes of deceit a capitalist and racist society brings down upon its underclasses. For a committed black writer, understanding the shape of the consciousness of Afro-Americans stimulates the direction that consciousness should take when formulating revolutionary political policy. "Bright and Morning Star," in short, identifies and conjoins the cultural means of Afro-Americans with the political ends of the Party to the benefit of both.

In order to bring together the cultural behaviors of Afro-Americans and the political aims of the Party, Wright paints his characters into a Marxian portrait of the South. Aunt Sue has lived in the post-slavery era, a time in which the white power structure holds blacks back from meaningful jobs, educational opportunities, and adequate wages. Emancipation has meant a new slavery: blacks in the South by and large are tenant farmers, laboring in corn and cotton fields they neither own nor control. Aunt Sue supports her alienated life by lugging bundles of white people's clothing to her home for washing and ironing. Some whites including Reva's parents are presumably as disinherited as Aunt Sue. Reva cries at one point because her brother is in jail, too, for organizing against the landowners' monopoly. A partially interdependent political movement among blacks and whites is apparent when Aunt Sue thinks " . . . outside in the rain were white and black, whom she had known all her life. Those people depended upon Johnny-Boy, loved him and looked to him as a man and leader" (167–168).

Afro-American survival in the South is based in the religious orientation of the black community. Afro-Americans have endured slavery with a culture that expressed work and religion similarly. "Long hours of scrubbing floors for a few cents a day had taught her who Jesus was, what a great boon it was to cling to Him, to be like Him and suffer without a mumbling word" (164). Wright says that

Aunt Sue's faith in Jesus and his suffering has led her to see a "wondrous vision" of a painless life in the future, but that vision has changed dramatically. She now recognizes the importance of surviving white abuse in a community more politically centered, more of this earth:

> . . . her sons had ripped from her startled eyes her old vision. . . . The wrongs and sufferings of black men had taken the place of Him nailed to the Cross; the meager beginnings of the party had become another Resurrection; and the hate of those who would destroy her new faith had quickened in her a hunger to feel how deeply her new strength went. (165)

But the suddenness of her second conversion belies a deeper notion: Aunt Sue may have a new faith but the hunger for freedom has always been there. That hunger permeates her life in the form of song which quite naturally comes to her lips whenever she labors methodically. The old hunger is always full of hope:

> Hes the Lily of the Valley, The Bright and Mawnin Star
> Hes the Fairest of Ten Thousan t mah soul . . . (163)

> He walks wid me,
> He talks wid me
> He tells me Ahm His own. . . .(164)

So strong is her faith that she wishes for a confrontation to test it, hoping that the whites will try to get the names of Party members out of her.

The test arrives as Aunt Sue undergoes a personal battle of loyalties over who to save and who not to betray. When Booker, a newcomer to the Party, comes to Aunt Sue to find out where Johnny-Boy and his friends are hiding, he tells her he only wants to protect them, to help them escape the Sheriff's gang. Johnny-Boy has told Aunt Sue she must trust those white members of the Party if they should come to her. "When folks pledge they word t be with us, then we gotta take em in. Wes too weak t be choosy" (170). So, in good faith, she divulges the identity of the comrades to Booker. His insistence makes her reason that she has acted wisely, but she feels the possibility of betrayal nonetheless. Then, as Reva arrives and tells her

Booker is a stoolie, Aunt Sue is horrified at what she's done. Wright extends the moment into one of his rare abstractions:

> Her having told the names of Johnny-Boy's comrades was but
> an incident in a deeper horror. She stood up and looked at the
> floor while call and counter-call, loyalty and counter-loyalty
> struggled in her soul. Mired she was between two abandoned
> worlds, living, but dying without the strength of the grace that
> either gave. (184)

Her conflict of loyalties, however, does not turn on whether to protect her son's life over those of his fellow workers, nor does it hinge on Johnny-Boy and his friends' protection from the Sheriff and the lynchers, although she acknowledges the Party members' needs. Essentially, Aunt Sue is protecting blacks, herself included, from the evil of whites. Although she fervently supports what her son believes, she, unlike him, does not fully trust the whites, in or out of the Party. For Aunt Sue the "white mountain" is everything. It manipulates her by the twin forces of kindness and deviousness. Reva, the white woman, loyal to Aunt Sue and in love with Johnny-Boy, embodies the kindness, and Aunt Sue recognizes her fidelity. But Booker, the slick-talking white who takes advantage of Johnny-Boy and Aunt Sue, embodies the deviousness. He plays on their gullibility. The CPUSA's intense push for racial equality also enables any white who says he is from the Party to ask for trust and thus gain an advantage. Promises, given and broken—it is the hypocritical tradition of Southern life, the essence of post-slavery platitudes and Jim Crow. The twin evils make her full embrace of a racially equal proletariat premature. As the old, endless hunger reasserts itself and ironically reasserts the old truth about whites, Aunt Sue quickly becomes deadlocked.

Trusting in the truth of her hunger is supposed to save her! However, for Aunt Sue, salvation and truth are not necessarily synonymous. Johnny-Boy's trust in all people—"Ah cant see white n Ah cant see black, Ah sees rich men n Ah sees po men" he says (171)—makes Aunt Sue's selective trust among whites she knows and doesn't know a virtue on which she is ultimately sacrificed. This fact decrees a terrible irony. While Johnny-Boy's comrades will be caught because of Aunt Sue's mistake, Aunt Sue learns that she has also betrayed her own vision, one which said that all whites except the Savior should be distrusted. She knows, after Reva unmasks Booker's identity, that she should have minded more her preoccupation with the impending doom she felt, minded her religious fatalism, not her son's goodwill to others. Once she has sacrificed her old vision for the new trust and that trust has turned sour, the only thing left for her is to synthesize the old and new visions by acting. She must try to warn Johnny-Boy. But more importantly, she must kill Booker before he tells the others who is in the Party. She must kill him to silence him so as the Party members will never know a white had finagled her trust. Her pride and her discernment are at stake. She must kill Booker in order to retrieve her pride and discernment, those elements of consciousness which her overzealous belief in the Party had forced her to let slip.

The sacrificial element for Aunt Sue comes about I believe because of the element of grace which prefigures it. Wright says that it was the "strength of grace" that allowed her to face the Sheriff's abuses, the grace a gift her sons and the Party had also given her. Aunt Sue is aware of the condition of grace from her Christian upbringing. Grace allows her to sacrifice herself because she knows that God's presence, mercy, and transformative powers are real. God lessened her burden, she feels. But it is faith which undoes her after the betrayal scene with Booker. In fact, understanding why her faith has failed her becomes her central conflict. She cannot understand why she must undergo the process of relearning what faith means. Of course she doesn't know it, but becoming conscious of the nature of trust and betrayal will show her. Indeed, she hopes now to understand her new faith not merely "have" it. Hope is the one emotion, the overwhelming emotion of "Bright and Morning Star," through which she can endure the contradictoriness of faith.

All of Aunt Sue's actions are based on a hope for something better. The old songs offer hope, Johnny-Boy's uncritical trust in whites offers hope, Reva and those whites in the Party she can fully trust offer hope. Even the revenge against Booker suggests a hopeful urgency that his death will save the Party. The condition of grace, the temporary respite from toil or being personally responsible for one's actions, expresses itself through hope: Aunt Sue will be saved if she hopes hard enough for salvation.

While her faith undergoes its test, hope and the condition of grace carry her through. Yet because she attributes a certain mortality to faith, it follows that perhaps she has power over the condition of grace, too. In the same way that Christianity graced her life with the concept of heaven, now she graces her own life with a heaven possible on earth. She realizes that by rewarding herself with Booker's blood, her actions can have consequences she directs. We feel the power of fate relinquish part of itself to Aunt Sue. She uses that power to create her own world through revolutionary action, where certainly in the South it is revolutionary for a black woman to kill a white man. She accepts her mental lapse and forgives herself by going after Booker. Consequently, as she replaces her old hunger, faith, vision, and hope with a new objective identity, based on her own actions, so, too, does she replace the agent of grace-giving: she becomes responsible for her own grace. This of course is not without cost to her.

Thus for Aunt Sue the grace of Christianity is transformed into the grace of a socialist vision; it means she will exercise more personal control over the moral dilemma the world has imposed upon her. Though she may decide her course, she has yet to witness it, and that thought is fearful enough in itself. She turns to hope again:

> The clearer she felt it the fuller did something well up from the depths of her for release; the more urgent did she feel the need to fling into her black sky another star, another hope, one more terrible vision to give her the strength to live and act. (184)

In Wright's didactic tones, the process of Afro-American, religious-based class consciousness should possess this intense give-and-take between the old and the new visions, with the old vision breaking back into the new. The suffering inherent in both world-views of Christianity and Marxism, Wright asserts should be exploited because the two are so close in their passionate self-righteousness.

Wright examines the religious nature of Aunt Sue's life and her final sacrifice in such detail, in such slowed motion, to show that what distinguishes her death is her recognition of her conscious life. What comes of that recognition from the Marxist perspective is that the consciousness leads to political acts.

However, the Party must see with such conscious vision, too. It must see the cultural processes of consciousness in order to know better those it would politically unify. Wright's message to the CPUSA states that as Aunt Sue's revolt uses her reliance on Christian suffering to propel her actions and inspire others, the Party should somehow find a way to acknowledge the usefulness of this suffering, in political terms. The Party should avow the religious basis of its constituency, that many of its members like Aunt Sue belong because of their utopian beliefs and their capacity through hope and suffering for acting continually on those beliefs. Even though the Party advances itself through political activity, it cannot reject the expressions of religious suffering, for those expressions, and not any political principles, may be the rivets which hold a people firmly together.

In the final chapter Wright further resolves the ethics of Aunt Sue's methods of survival with the tactical strength of the Party. Aunt Sue now re-uses Afro-American traditions of striking back against whites but to the Party's benefit. What she felt as her counter-loyalty to the Party, acting naturally against the ages old trickery of whites, resurfaces as resistance on behalf of whites and blacks in an integrated CPUSA. When Aunt Sue goes after Booker by playing dumb and hiding a gun under a white sheet the Sheriff had sarcastically told her to bring as a shroud, she is "puttin' on massa," true to the old Afro-American feigned ploy to gain some advantage over an aggressor. When she shoots Booker she proves that by having trusted a white, having talked to Booker, it was actually a way to save whites, those "right" whites in the movement. Thus, by using her deference as a political maneuver, she wields it to the Party's advantage and she vindicates her traditions, too. This tactic gains further credence once Aunt Sue, Johnny-Boy and Booker are dead, and the anonymity of the remaining comrades is presumably preserved. This often overlooked resolution in the plot means that Aunt Sue's final conscious act unifies the Party and grants it a legacy.

But a hard fact remains. Aunt Sue is able to save whites—the partisans—only after she has killed one. Presumably she is the only one in the Party who knows Booker has deceived her, but that is not the point of her action. The point for her was to be vindicated: Booker's death was more correct to her because he was white. To understand this, imagine if you will that Booker was black—there probably would have been no deceit whatsoever or, if there were, the Sheriff could not have compared one black person's word with another's as easily as he did. From the Afro-American perspective, Booker's deceit represents a mountain of injustice. It underscores the necessity that the death of racist whites is essential to Afro-American freedom, a freedom from white coercion that blacks require alongside economic emancipation.

When Aunt Sue dies in the final, brutal scene, Wright says of her "She gave up as much of her life as she could before they took it from her" (192). The purposely unclear referent for "they" has a wonderful resonance. It is a "they" of the whites, the deception, the sweet-talk, the Sheriff's intimidation; but it also includes a "they" of the Party, the comrades, her sons, the cultural patterns of her community. Both "they"'s receive Aunt Sue's life for she gives it to become conscious of her own faith and its social purpose as well as to teach others the same thing. As she retains as much control as possible over her death, it testifies to Aunt Sue's wish that the revolution proceed for Afro-Americans in the direction she has charted.

"Bright and Morning Star" shows that Afro-Americans are caught between these two opposing referents, between trusting whites and betraying their conscientious protection of the black community. This is an antagonism they bear in themselves and in the community, but it is not authorized by their culture. Rather, it stems from methods whites have used to make blacks defer to them.

The idea of deference as it relates to different uses by black and white is complicated in the story and requires sorting out. When Aunt Sue defers to Booker, she is acting obediently, answering when spoken to; *not* answering has traditionally been met with a whip. When Aunt Sue comes to the Sheriff with a shroud, she not only defers obediently she also answers as a way of gaining her own advantage, to get close enough to kill Booker. And when Johnny-Boy says Aunt Sue must believe whites, he defers for the sake of a political expedient. Johnny-Boy wants to trust whites because it is a way of making the Party grow more cohesive. Depending upon the agent and goal, deference has positive and negative uses.

But whites, in or out of the Party, face in themselves or their communities no such deferential acts. This is because deference arises in blacks from the inequalities they have faced under the thumb of the class system. Because blacks in order to survive retain the slave roles of master and servant as tactical maneuvers and "natural" behaviors years after their "emancipation," some think that blacks' deference has a basis in the racial difference between black and white. Nothing could be more ludicrous. But maintaining the myth of a certain "racial" behavior like deference continues to empower the class system. The system uses the old slave attitudes to enforce differences, which, in turn, continues to isolate social groups and institutionalize differences between races.

To survive, the class system requires a hierarchy of different levels of value. Obedience historically repeated over and over forces one group into the role of an underclass even without the law of slavery to justify it.

Black culture uses the behavior of deference occasionally to its advantage as a way of undermining whites' control, avoiding a fight, saving a life. But more often, the ways Afro-Americans must kowtow to whites result in blacks distrusting themselves, questioning their motives, and always wondering what paradox of kindness and deceit the white person is offering.

Aunt Sue's distrust of her own actions even when she is asked to trust another person is precisely the sort of conditioned response she has learned from the world at large. However, Aunt Sue realizes that deferring to Booker actually released her own logic about the nature of deference. She practices and unlearns a part of her culture that both proffers both trust and betrayal as cohesive factors in the culture. She never ceases to fight her victimization whether it resides in the black community's response to oppression or in the white's abuse of that response.

Wright is describing the constant predicament for Afro-Americans: what to believe when everything from racial differences to cultural identity appears manipulated. Aunt Sue sees the totality of this manipulation, notably in how blacks are trained to defer and how they use it to their advantage. She dies, a symbol of a total consciousness that Wright wishes her "class" of a person to represent. Coming to this total view, she liberates a perspective the entire working class needs to recognize, for its members must see (and be shown) into the deepest class-based system of any manipulation. In short, as blacks unveil the consciousness about whites in which they have been reared, then whites presumably see the patterns of abuse they have practiced, particularly within the working class or among those of the intellectual left. If the goal is to root out of the system its learned biases, how better than to be instructed by those who know its abuses best.

Class consciousness then in "Bright and Morning Star" comes through cultural strength and conscious political action. Christianity is not a foe of Marxism but has useful, tactical strains that help define the direction of revolutionary consciousness. The religious life of the community itself manipulates people's behavior, but not in the way that the class system creates the conditions in which a religion or a culture are processed and in which elements of trust and betrayal become part of the system's apparatus of control. Blacks have to show whites how the class system twists the meanings of racial difference, trust, and deference in order that everyone realize how deep racism has affected black religious and political visions. Wright has not placed Afro-American cultural needs above class solidarity (as Calmer claimed) but has shown that the character of their cultural expressions serves with its visionary integrity, its faith, the utopian spirit that the working class needs. By examining the process of learning and unlearning deference, Wright further finds less antagonism between black and white and more between the partisan and the racist *white* who, in terms of their solidarity, have many more problems to overcome. Wright achieves a great synthesis with his story: he directs us within Afro-American life to the place where the different paths of its religious-centered culture, its conditioned deference to whites, and its need for a working-class political vision can meet.

"Bright and Morning Star" complexly vindicated the communist cause, and the work proved most critics on the Left were quite far from understanding the deeper political links between race, culture, and class that Wright knew were apparent in black life. Aunt Sue's life and death are complex but politically unequivocal. Her passion gives birth to a revolutionary socialism effective for the present age, without fear of whites, for their deaths are not counterproductive but liberating for both black and white, and without mystical foundations, for humankind can replace Christ without necessarily losing its utopian strength. Why this mix of agit-prop and literary merit has not been found in other leftist writers of the 1930s is perplexing. Perhaps more sociological analysis of class and culture in fiction will show what the literature has already demonstrated.

References

Baldwin, James. *The Fire Next Time*. New York: Dell Publishing Co., 1962, 1963.

Calmer, Alan. *New York Daily Worker*, April 4, 1938, 7.

DuBois, W. E. Burghardt. *The Souls of Black Folk*, 1903. New York: Fawcett Publications, 1961.

Hicks, Granville. *Granville Hicks in The New Masses.* Ed. Jack Alan Robbins. Port Washington, N. Y.: Kennikat Press, 1981.

Klein, Marcus. *Foreigners: The Making of American Literature 1900–1940.* Chicago: The University of Chicago Press, 1981.

Margolies, Edward. "The Short Stories: Uncle Tom's Children; Eight Men." *Critical Essays on Richard Wright.* Ed. Yoshinobu Hakutani. Boston: G.K. Hall & Co., 1982.

Wright, Richard. *Uncle Tom's Children*, 1938. New York: Signet Books, 1947.

Index